Salman El-Farsi

(SALMAN THE PERSIAN)

D1553869

A short story of his life

by

Sayed A. A. Razwy

TAHRIKE TARSILE QUR'AN, INC.
PUBLISHERS AND DISTRIBUTORS OF HOLY QUR'AN
P.O. Box 1115, Corona-Elmhurst Sta.
Elmhurst, N.Y. 11373-1115

Published by
Tahrike Tarsile Qur'an, Inc.
Publishers and Distributors of Holy Qur'an
P.O. Box 1115
Corona-Elmhurst Station
Elmhurst, New York 11373-1115

Second U.S. Edition 1988

Library of Congress Catalog Number: 87-051616
British Library Cataloguing in Publication Data
ISBN: 0-940368-83-8

Distributors in United States:

Anjumane Aza Khana-E-Zahra
1365 Exeter Street
Baldwin, N.Y. 11510

Distributors in Europe:

Mihrab Publishers & Book Distributors
20 Potters Lane, Kiln Farm
Milton Keynes, MK11 3HF, U.K.

Distributors in Canada:

Mihrab Publishers & Book Distributors Canada
36 Robbinstone Drive
Scarborough, Ontario
Canada M1B 2E6

Salman El-Farsi

(SALMAN THE PERSIAN)

A short story of his life

by

Sayed A. A. Razwy

TABLE OF CONTENTS

INTRODUCTION

Salman the Persian was one of the companions of Muhammed Mustafa, the Last and the Greatest Messenger of Allah on this earth (may Allah bless him and his Ahlel-Bayt). As a companion of Muhammed Mustafa, he was pre-eminent among the eminent. But the story of his life, unlike the story of the lives of most of the other companions of Muhammed, the blessed one, is hidden in mystery. Very little is known about it. This is strange, considering his high rank in the sight of Muhammed Mustafa - his master in the two worlds - and his rapturous orientation with Islam. The events of his life, it appears, are still awaiting some future seeker of Truth, to come and to uncover them.

A modest attempt has been made in the pages of this book to depict the life of Salman the Persian from sources which were readily available. It puts the focus on his love of Allah, his unflagging quest for the eternal truths; his "discovery" of Islam and his allegiance to it; his devotion to Muhammed Mustafa, the Messenger of Allah; and his irrevocable "alignment" with Justice, Truth and Simplicity.

Salman's story is an integral part of the devotional and inspirational heritage of Islam, and it's a poignant study of the manner in which he demonstrated the application of the principles of Islam to his personal and public life. He was a witness, par excellence, of the Truth and Sublimity of those principles. He also made a rich and a most compelling contribution to the story of the religious perception and experience of all mankind.

May Allah be pleased with His loving slave, Salman the Persian. He personified obedience to Allah, and devotion to Muhammed Mustafa (*may Allah bless him and his Ahlel-Bayt*).

Chapter I

The Companionship of Muhammed Mustafa (S) and Salman El- Farsi (R)

The Arab historians have estimated the total number of the "companions" or "friends" of Muhammed Mustafa, the Messenger of Allah (may Allah bless him and his Ahlel-Bayt), at 150,000. Their definition of a companion or a friend of Muhammed Mustafa, the Prophet of Islam, is any Muslim who saw him with his own eyes. But this definition lacks precision. It is like stating that an American saw the President of the United States at a political rally or in a motorcade, and waved at him. Perhaps the President also noticed him, and waved back at him, and this act of seeing each other or being seen by each other, makes both of them "friends" of each other.

In the case of our Prophet (may Allah bless him and his Ahlel-Bayt), it is entirely possible that 150,000 Muslims saw him with their own eyes. But it should be borne in mind that many among these Muslims were youngsters, and some were even children. Many others among them were fresh converts to Islam, and since most of them were illiterate Bedouins, their knowledge of the Articles of Faith and the Principles of Islam, or of the character, personality and mission of the Prophet, was minimal. Perhaps it didn't extend beyond their ability to repeat the Shahadah (=the declaration that God is One, and Muhammed is His Messenger). Still others "accepted" Islam but their sincerity in doing so, was open to question. In fact, the sincerity of their faith

3

was questioned, not by their contemporaries, but by Quran Majid - the Book of Allah - itself, as we read in the following verse:

THE DESERT ARABS SAY: "WE BELIEVE."
SAY: "YE HAVE NO FAITH: BUT YE (ONLY) SAY,
'WE HAVE SUBMITTED OUR WILLS TO ALLAH.'
FOR FAITH HAS NOT YET ENTERED YOUR HEARTS."

(Chapter 49; verse 14)

But Quran Majid was not content merely with questioning the faith of the Arabs; it also had many other reservations about them, and it was unequivocal in expressing them as and when the occasion arose.

There were, for example, those Arabs who believed that by accepting Islam, they had placed Muhammed, the Messenger of Allah, under an obligation to themselves. Perhaps they expected him to acknowledge his "indebtedness" to them for accepting Islam. But Quran Majid didn't agree with them, and said about them:

THEY IMPRESS ON THEE AS A FAVOR THAT THEY
HAVE EMBRACED ISLAM.
SAY: COUNT NOT YOUR ISLAM AS A FAVOR UPON
ME.
NAY, ALLAH HAS CONFERRED A FAVOR UPON YOU
THAT HE HAS GUIDED YOU TO THE FAITH,
IF YE BE TRUE AND SINCERE.

(Chapter 49; verse 17)

* * * * *

Some companions of Muhammed Mustafa, the Messenger of Allah, were too easily distracted by the craze for some petty gain or amusement. They could leave him standing alone in the act of

4

praying in the mosque for the sake of closing a business deal or for watching some passing show. About them we read in Quran:

BUT WHEN THEY SEE SOME BARGAIN OR SOME AMUSEMENT, THEY DISPERSE HEADLONG TO IT, AND LEAVE THEE STANDING (ALONE). SAY: "THE (BLESSING) FROM THE PRESENCE OF ALLAH IS BETTER THAN ANY AMUSEMENT OR BARGAIN! AND ALLAH IS THE BEST TO PROVIDE (FOR ALL NEEDS)."

(Chapter 62; verse 11)

Quran has also taken notice of those Muslims in Medina who loved their own lives more than they loved the life of the Messenger of Allah. If his life was in peril, they could desert him, perhaps without any remorse or pangs of conscience. Quran has pointedly reminded them that:

IT IS NOT FITTING FOR THE PEOPLE OF MEDINA AND THE BEDOUIN ARABS OF THE NEIGHBORHOOD, TO REFUSE TO FOLLOW ALLAH'S APOSTLE, NOR TO PREFER THEIR OWN LIVES TO HIS...

(Chapter 9; verse 120)

* * * * *

One of the most important duties of the Muslims was to wage Jihad, i.e., to fight in defence of Faith, and in defence of the Community of the Faithful. But it was a duty the zeal for which was not shared equally by all companions of the Prophet of Islam. Among them, there were those who were only tepidly interested in fighting against the enemies of Faith. About them Quran says:

5

*JUST AS THY LORD ORDERED THEE OUT OF
THY HOUSE IN TRUTH, EVEN THOUGH A PARTY
AMONG THE BELIEVERS DISLIKED IT. DISPUTING
WITH THEE CONCERNING THE TRUTH AFTER
IT WAS MADE MANIFEST, AS IF THEY WERE
BEING DRIVEN TO DEATH AND THEY
ACTUALLY SAW IT.*

(Chapter 8; verses 5 and 6)

Translator's Note:

Some of the Believers disputed concerning the "truth." They did not feel sure that the course recommended, was the true and right course. They thought it would be certain destruction: they saw death almost staring them in the face (A. Yusuf Ali).

If the companions could desert Muhammed Mustafa, the Messenger of Allah, while he was praying in the Mosque, they could also abandon him while he was fighting in the battle-field. Most of them bolted from the battle-field of Uhud to save their own lives. Following is the account of Quran on their performance in the battle of Uhud:

*BEHOLD! YE WERE CLIMBING UP THE
HIGH GROUND, WITHOUT EVEN CASTING A
SIDE GLANCE AT ANY ONE,
AND THE APOSTLE IN YOUR REAR WAS
CALLING YOU BACK.
THERE DID ALLAH GIVE YOU ONE
DISTRESS AFTER ANOTHER
BY WAY OF REQUITAL, TO TEACH YOU
NOT TO GRIEVE FOR (THE BOOTY)
THAT HAD ESCAPED YOU AND FOR (THE ILL)
THAT HAD BEFALLEN YOU.
FOR ALLAH IS WELL AWARE OF ALL THAT YE DO.*

(Chapter 3; verse 153)

And then there were the brazen "Muslims." Their brazenness was matched only by the brazenness of the infidels. They did not flinch even from such a hideous act like making an attempt to kill Muhammed Mustafa himself, even though he was their greatest benefactor. A modern reader would find it incredible that a Muslim, no matter how depraved, would ever contemplate such a crime. And yet, those "Muslims" went beyond contemplating the crime; they actually made the attempt. Following is the testimony of Quran Majid on the subject:

THEY SWEAR BY ALLAH THAT THEY SAID NOTHING (EVIL), BUT INDEED THEY UTTERED BLASPHEMY, AND THEY DID IT AFTER ACCEPTING ISLAM: AND THEY MEDITATED A PLOT WHICH THEY WERE UNABLE TO CARRY OUT: THIS REVENGE OF THEIRS WAS (THEIR) ONLY RETURN FOR THE BOUNTY WITH WHICH ALLAH AND HIS APOSTLE HAD ENRICHED THEM...

(Chapter 9; verse 74)

Translator's Note:

The reference here is to a plot made by the Apostle's enemies to kill him when he was returning from Tabuk. It was all the more dastardly in that some of the conspirators were among the men of Medina, who were enriched by the general prosperity that followed the peace and good government established through Islam in Medina. Trade flourished, justice was firmly administered with an even hand. And the only return these men could make was a return of evil for good. That was their revenge, because Islam aimed at suppressing selfishness, stood for the rights of the poorest and humblest and judged worth by righteousness rather than by birth or position. (A. Yusuf Ali).

The times of Muhammed Mustafa, the Messenger of Allah, were, without a question, the best and the most blessed of times. But this does not mean that the people living in those times, were all saints and angels. Of course, there were many saintly, angelic, pious and God-fearing men and women among them; but also among them, there were the sycophants, the opportunists, the parasites, and the tuft-hunters. These latter have been designated by Quran Majid as Munafiqeen (=Hypocrites).

These Munafiqeen had declared themselves to be Muslims but they had done so with many mental reservations. By their duplicity and double-talk, they had earned for themselves the most stinging broadsides in Quran Majid, which, inevitably, had made them very conspicuous. They were conspicuous, not only by their quality but also by their quantity. (1) But when Muhammed Mustafa, the Messenger of Allah, died, they also "disappeared" from the scene. Their disappearance synchronized with the death of Muhammed Mustafa, may Allah bless him and his Ahlel-Bayt.

(1) M. Shibli, the Indian historian of Islam, says in his biography of Hadhrat Umar ibn al-Khattab, the second khalifa of the Muslims, that at the death of Muhammed Mustafa, "Medina was full of Munafiqeen. They were awaiting an opportune moment (such as the death of Muhammed Mustafa), to strike a death blow to Islam..." (Al-Farooq).

The sinister and unwelcome presence of the Munafiqeen in Medina, was attested, repeatedly and most emphatically, by Quran Majid, and yet their "disappearance" went totally unnoticed. It's incredible but true that it did not occur to anyone in Medina to ask where did the Munafiqeen go.

No one would suggest that the death of Muhammed Mustafa, may Allah bless him and his Ahlel-Bayt, was the signal the Munafiqeen were awaiting to become sincere and devout Muslims. Actually, they had not "disappeared." They were all present in Medina, watching the drift of events, taking stock of the new situation, and hatching plans to manipulate it.

During the lifetime of Muhammed Mustafa - the recipient of revelation from Heaven - the Munafiqeen had lived in constant fear of being mortified by Quran Majid, as they frequently were. About their fear we read in Quran as follows:

THE HYPOCRITES ARE AFRAID LEST A SURA (CHAPTER) SHOULD BE SENT DOWN ABOUT THEM, SHOWING THEM WHAT IS IN THEIR HEARTS...
(Chapter 9; verse 64)

But the death of Muhammed Mustafa, the blessed Messenger of Allah, freed the Munafiqeen from fear of indictment by Quran. His death "invested" them with a new sense of "security," and assurance. And since they were "pragmatic" men, they took the simple step of "blending" - quietly and imperceptibly - into the general body of Muslims. In fact, they did better; they changed their status from Munafiqeen (Hypocrites or nominal Muslims) to Momineen (true believers). The Muslim society in Medina then became a "crucible" in which all distinction was lost between the genuine and the fake Muslims, and it became impossible to identify, much less to isolate, the latter.

But the judgment of Quran has consistently been stern and severe on the Munafiqeen (=Hypocrites). Some of its verses in which it occurs, are as follows:

THE HYPOCRITES WILL BE IN
THE LOWEST DEPTHS OF FIRE...
(Chapter 4; verse 145)

* * * * *

ALLAH HATH PROMISED THE HYPOCRITES,
MEN AND WOMEN,
AND THE REJECTERS OF FAITH,

9

THE FIRE OF HELL:
THEREIN SHALL THEY DWELL:
SUFFICIENT IS IT FOR THEM:
FOR THEM IS THE CURSE OF ALLAH,
AND AN ENDURING PUNISHMENT.

(Chapter 9; verse 68)

* * * * *

CERTAIN OF THE DESERT ARABS
ROUND ABOUT YOU ARE HYPOCRITES,
AS WELL AS (DESERT ARABS)
AMONG THE MEDINA FOLK:
THEY ARE OBSTINATE IN HYPOCRISY:
THOU KNOWEST THEM NOT: WE KNOW THEM:
TWICE SHALL WE PUNISH THEM:
AND IN ADDITION SHALL THEY
BE SENT TO A GRIEVOUS PENALTY.

(Chapter 9; verse 101)

All these men whose portrait Quran Majid has drawn in the verses quoted in the foregoing pages, were Muslims, and they had seen Muhammed Mustafa, not once but on countless occasions. They probably saw him many times every day. After all, many of them gathered in the Great Mosque to say their prayers behind him five times every day.

Without a doubt, it was one of the greatest blessings and honors for a Muslim to have seen the Last and the Greatest Messenger of Allah on this earth, with his own eyes. But friendship with him called for a few other requirements also such as a Muslim's unquestioning obedience to Allah, and transcendental love for him (for Muhammed Mustafa). Without obedience to Allah and love for His Messenger, such a claim would only be a burlesque of friendship.

A companion or friend of Muhammed Mustafa (may Allah bless him and his Ahlel-Bayt), would have to be more than a mere (Muslim) contemporary of his. He would have to be a man with a firm commitment to uphold the ideals of Islam, and a proven ability, or, at least, a resolve to strengthen the mission of its Prophet. He would also have to be ready, willing and able, to offer material sacrifices, and if necessary, to offer his own life, as well as the lives of his loved ones, as sacrifice, in the defence of Islam. For such a man, it would not even be necessary to have "seen" Muhammed Mustafa with his own eyes. He would qualify for the honor of the companionship of Muhammed Mustafa even without seeing him with his own eyes. There was such a man. His name was Owais Qarni, and he lived in Yemen. He loved Muhammed Mustafa such as few others ever did, and he was eager to sacrifice his fortune, his limbs and his life - all for Islam. May Allah be pleased with him. He was a bosom friend of Muhammed Mustafa, and yet the two never met each other.

Conversely, mere physical propinquity with Muhammed Mustafa was no guarantee that a companion's faith would be invulnerable to temptations of any kind. Notwithstanding his propinquity with Muhammed Mustafa, he could be just as liable to deviate from the prescriptions of Islam as a non-companion. But in his case, deviation would only be much more reprehensible.

It would be quite logical to assume that the crude impulses and the primitive instincts of the Arabs were sublimated in the company of Muhammed Mustafa, the Messenger of Allah. It would, therefore, be just as logical to assume that they - the Muslim contemporaries of Muhammed Mustafa - were models of excellence. Many of them were. But not everyone! Among them, there were those men who lapsed from excellence. Following examples will make this point clear.

One of the Muslims claiming that he was a friend of Muhammed Mustafa (may Allah bless him and his Ahlel-Bayt), was Hassan

11

ibn Thabit. He was the "press agent" of the Prophet, and the "poet laureate" at his court in Medina. He figured very prominently in the scandal called the *"incident of ifk."*

The incident of ifk took place in December 626 when the Prophet of Islam was returning to Medina from a campaign. Hadhrat Ayesha who was one of his wives, had accompanied him in the campaign. She was inadvertently left behind when the army marched out of its camp, and some of the Munafiqeen (=hypocrites) seized the opportunity, to smudge her reputation. One of the companions who joined the scandal-mongers in the character-assassination of Ayesha, was Hassan ibn Thabit - the court poet of the Prophet himself.

Later, a verse was revealed vindicating Hadhrat Ayesha, and Hassan ibn Thabit had to pay the penalty of maliciously spreading gross imputations. His misdemeanor was not condoned because of his status as a companion of the Prophet. Muhammad Husayn Haykal writes in his book, *The Life of Muhammed* (Cairo, 1935), that Hassan ibn Thabit was "brought into the marketplace, and was flogged 80 stripes."

No companion or friend of the Prophet of Islam could presume on his position. In the egalitarian society of Islam, a companion (or a non-companion) could stand or fall strictly on the merit (or lack of it) of his deeds.

Another incident showing want of restraint or lack of inhibitions in a companion of the Prophet of Islam, took place in A.D. 628 in Hudaybiyya. Amin Dawidar, the Egyptian historian, writes in his book, *Suwar Min Hayat er-Rasul* (Pictures From the Life of the Prophet), (Cairo, 1953), about it, as follows:

> In February 628, Muhammed, the Messenger of Allah, signed a treaty of peace with the pagans of Makkah. The treaty had just been signed when a young Makkan, newly converted to Islam, escaped from captivity in Makkah, arrived in the Muslim camp,

12

and sought asylum. He was loaded in chains, and he begged the Messenger of Allah to take him under his protection.

There was a heart-rending scene. Muhammed had given a pledge to repatriate any Muslim escaping from Makkah. If he had taken the fugitive under his protection, his position in the sight of the pagans would have been compromised. This he could not allow. The fugitive, therefore, had to be turned away, much to the chagrin and mortification of the Muslims.

The Prophet then left Hudaybiyya to return to Medina. He was at one or two days journey from Makkah when a new chapter of Quran, called Sura-tul-Fath (=Victory), was revealed to him from Heaven. In this chapter, the Treaty of Hudaybiyya was called "the Manifest Victory."

Muhammed Mustafa, the Messenger of Allah (may Allah bless him and his Ahlel-Bayt), assembled the Muslims, and read to them the new revelation which begins with the following verse:

VERILY, WE HAVE GRANTED THEE
A MANIFEST VICTORY.

(Chapter 48, verse 1)

But some of the Muslim were still in a sullen and a resentful mood. They could not see the Treaty of Hudaybiyya as "a Manifest Victory." One of them tartly observed: "This is not a victory. We have been prevented from entering the House (Kaaba), and Muhammed has turned away a believer who had sought sanctuary from him."

These remarks were brought to the attention of the Prophet, and he said: "What a foul speech! Yes, this (the Treaty of Hudaybiyya) is the greatest of victories..."

The companion in this story, whose name has not been disclosed by Amin Dawidar, apparently believed that the Treaty of

Hudaybiyya lacked such components as prudence, foresight and perspicacity. He was disagreeing, not only with the Messenger of Allah, but with Allah Himself Who called the Treaty of Hudaybiyya "the Manifest Victory" in His Book, which in fact it was, as events were very soon to show.

The companions of Muhammed Mustafa (may Allah bless him and his Ahlel-Bayt), also had to work, like any other people, to make a living for themselves and their families. Thus the Muhajireen (the Immigrants from Makkah) were, for the most part, traders, merchants and peddlers. The Ansar (the Supporters; the citizens of Medina), were mostly farmers. In both groups, there were craftsmen such as carpenters, blacksmiths, weavers, tailors, masons, shoemakers etc. There were also unskilled workers such as porters and shepherds, and everyone of them found a niche for himself in the economic life of Medina.

One of the companions of Muhammed Mustafa who was a late-comer into the ranks of the Muslims, was Abu Hurayra. He accepted Islam in A.D. 629 but he probably decided not to do anything to make a living. He figured that he would be more comfortable if he fed himself from the *sadaqat* (charity) of the Muslims. He was thus able to free himself from the anxieties and problems of earning a competence.

Once Abu Hurayra made his decision to live on welfare, he had unlimited leisure at hand. He utilized his leisure hours by spending them in the court of the Prophet of Islam where he knew that he would always find something to eat. The Prophet, of course, never turned him or anyone else away from his door, hungry.

But Abu Hurayra was so much in the presence of the Prophet of Islam that he made himself almost "obtrusive."

Muhammed Mustafa (may Allah bless him and his Ahlel Bayt) was well-known for his courtesy and condescension. In some matters, he was excessively fastidious. For example, he did not like to hurt anyone's feelings. And yet, he felt constrained to quote before Abu Hurayra, the Arabian equivalent of the English adage: Absences make the heart grow fonder. In other words, Muhammed Mustafa, the Messenger of Allah, suggested to him to put some intervals between his visits.But the Prophet's remark was too subtle, and Abu Hurayra did not understand its purport.

In later times, Abu Hurayra revealed a great flair for narrating the Hadith (=the traditions of the Prophet of Islam), and became famous for his contributions to the Hadith literature. He probably narrated more Hadith than any other companion of the Prophet. There was never an occasion when recollection did not come to him of something that the Messenger of Allah had said to him. Gibbon, the historian, says in his *Decline and Fall of the Roman Empire* that Hadith narrated by Abu Hurayra require corroboration.

* * * * *

This should also be borne in mind by the students of the early history of Islam that there was no such thing in Medina, after the death of Muhammed Mustafa (may Allah bless him and his Ahlel-Bayt), as a ",test" of one's faith, or, a "censor" of the personal conduct and character of the people who had seen him. Therefore, anyone could claim that he was his (the Prophet's) companion or friend, without any fear of being challenged as to his "credentials" for such companionship or friendship. After the conquest of Makkah, too many of his (the Prophet's) contemporaries were candidates for that honor. Some of them, without a doubt, wished to ingratiate themselves with him. And after his death, the only way some of them could make themselves important in the sight of others, was to claim that they were his companions.

The definition of a "companion" of Muhammed Mustafa, the

15

Messenger of Allah, as a Muslim who saw him with his own eyes, is, as we have seen, too loose, and is, therefore, unsatisfactory. We have, therefore, to find another definition of the term "companion of Muhammed."

There could probably be many definitions but I think that the most logical definition of a companion of Muhammed, the Messenger of Allah, would be a man whom he (Muhammed Mustafa) himself called his companion. The choice of companions and friends should be left to him. He could pick and choose them better than anyone else. If he did not call a man his companion, then the latter's claim to his (Muhammed's) companionship could have no meaning. Muhammed Mustafa did not call and could not call 150,000 men his companions. He probably never even saw most of them, and with many of them he had perhaps little more than a nodding acquaintance, and with still others, he perhaps did nothing more than exchange a greeting, and that too not more than once.

But there were those men who were the companions and friends of Muhammed Mustafa (may Allah bless him and his Ahlel-Bayt). They were his companions and friends because he chose them for the honor of his companionship and friendship. Not only they loved him; he also loved them. They were remarkable men, and their love for him was just as remarkable. It was remarkable, among other things, for its consistency. It was love that never faltered. They loved him because they knew that he was the perfect one; the infallible one. And they loved him because they knew that he was the loved one of Allah. It was their glorious destiny to be the members of the "team" which under his leadership, laid the foundations of the Kingdom of Heaven on Earth. Their sacrifices, their tenacity, their courage and their dedication to duty were to be the underpinnings of that Kingdom. Quran Majid itself paid its tributes to them in the

16

following verse:

*THE VANGUARD (OF ISLAM) - THE FIRST OF THOSE
WHO FORESOOK (THEIR HOMES) AND OF THOSE
WHO GAVE THEM AID, AND (ALSO) THOSE WHO
FOLLOW THEM IN (ALL) GOOD DEEDS, -
WELL-PLEASED IS ALLAH WITH THEM, AS
THEY ARE WITH HIM, FOR THEM HATH HE
PREPARED GARDENS UNDER WHICH
RIVERS FLOW, TO DWELL THEREIN FOR EVER:
THAT IS THE SUPREME FELICITY*

(Chapter 9; verse 100)

These men - the companions and friends of Muhammed Mustafa - had won the pleasure of Allah. There is not, and there cannot be a greater honor for a mortal in this world or in theHereafter, than to win the pleasure of Allah. Allah bestowed accolades upon them in His Book. He was "well-pleased" with them.

But these recipients of the accolades of Heaven, were, in the nature of things, very few in number, and they belonged to the select group of the favorites of Muhammed Mustafa, the Messenger of Allah (may Allah bless him and his Ahlel-Bayt). One of them, and one who was a greater favorite of his than most of them, was Salman el-Farsi - Salman the Persian. May Allah be pleased with him, and may He bless him.

Salman el-Farsi was truly extraordinary in the entire entourage of Muhammed Mustafa, the beloved Messenger of Allah. He wrote a stirring chapter in the epic of Islam on the love of Allah and His Messenger. This book is a synopsis of that chapter.

Chapter II

Early Years in Persia (Iran)

According to the investigations and researches of the Arab historians, Salman was born in or around the year A.D. 568, in a small town in Persia (Iran) called Jiyye. The modern city of Isfahan stands on the site of Jiyye. Incidentally, Salman was not the name given to him at his birth. His Persian name was Rozeba. Many years later when he became a Muslim, his master, Muhammed Mustafa, the Messenger of Allah (may Allah bless him and his Ahlel-Bayt), changed his name to Salman. During the years when he was at the court of his master, Muhammed Mustafa, he was, sometimes, also addressed, by his friends, as Abu Abdullah (=the father of Abdullah).

Salman's father was a rich landlord and a powerful political figure in Jiyye and the surrounding areas. He had much property in the city, and vast estates in the country, and he had numerous slaves and many herds of horses. Since Salman was his only child, he lavished all his love upon him. If Salman went out for playing with other children, the slaves of his father chaperoned him. His father's orders to them were not to let him get out of their sight at any time.

* * * * *

Most Persians (=Iranians) in those days were Magians (1) or

18

Zoroastrians, i.e., they were the followers of the Persian prophet, Zoroaster. Salman was also taught the principles and doctrines of Magianism or Zoroastrianism. He was an incredibly precocious child, and exhibited amazing interest in and ability at assimilating new knowledge. He was in his early teens when he grasped the highly complex, sometimes esoteric, doctrines and dogmas of theology, mysticism and philosophy as well as the recondite ideas of the Persian national belief in the cosmic war between Light and Darkness, Truth and Falsehood, Good and Evil, and Right and Wrong. Soon he knew as much as his own teachers and the priests of the Zoroastrian fire temple in Jiyye did.

(1) Magian (Majus) have been mentioned in Quran Majid in verse 17 of the 22nd chapter (Surat-ul-Hajj). They consider fire as the purest and the noblest element, and worship it as a fit emblem of God. Their location was the Persian and Median uplands and the Mesopotamian valley (Iraq). Their religion was reformed by the Prophet Zoroaster (circa 600 B.C.). Their scripture is the Zend-Avesta, the Bible of the Parsis. They were the "wise men of the East" mentioned in the Gospels. (A. Yusuf Ali).

In those days in Persia, it was considered a great honor to be a priest in one of the fire-temples. Priesthood was one of the "blue-ribbon" careers open to young men of ambition, and many of them were attracted to it. Service in a fire-temple provided the priests with more than a mere competence. It brought them status, dignity, prestige and numerous perquisites. It will be remembered that in the social organization of India also, the highest honors were reserved for the class of the priests called the Brahmins. In ancient Egypt, during the period of the 21st dynasty, the clergy of Amon in Thebes established the "Dynasty of the Priest-Kings." When these Priest-Kings died, they were apotheosized, and their subjects worshipped them. And according to the Roman catechism of 1567, priests are called not only angels but "gods," because "they are the holders among us, of the power and the might of the Immortal God." The Catholic clergy was not, by any means, disdainful of political power either. Many cardinals became prime ministers of Spain, France and England.

Since in Persia also, the priests could reach high positions in local and "national" governments, Salman's father managed to get him appointed as a priest in the local fire-temple while he was only sixteen years old. He perhaps hoped to use the fire-temple as a "spring-board" to launch his highly-gifted son on a political career.

Salman thus became one of the priests or guardians of the fire-temple of Jiyye. The temple was a landmark of Jiyye, obviously designed to accommodate people as well as to please the eye. The local architects had expended all their talents and skills in making it beautiful. It was Salman's duty, each morning, to open its gates, to check maintenance, and to assign duties to the crew. In the evening he returned, with other priests, to conduct the service. The temple, now bedecked with flowers and shimmering with candles, inspired deep feelings of reverence in the worshippers. Salman burnt incense, and fed the sacred fire with sandalwood. Columns of scented smoke curled up from the temple's chimneys toward the sky. People came for adorations from far and near. Fire, for them, was a symbol of purity; it had the power to burn away all dross. The devout among them brought rich and exotic gifts with them like frankincense and myrrh or pieces of gold or ancient heirlooms and many-splendored stones. The craftsmanship of some of these oblations amazed Salman, and the fire of the stones dazzled him. He especially admired one stone which looked like the living heart of light. There was a blue stone which he thought, was a fragment of the mid-summer night sky. His other "favorites" included a stone which, he believed, held captive a ray of sunrise. Another stone was vivid like a flame, and there was a crystal which was transparent and pure like a spear of ice.

In the beginning, Salman was happy at his job, and he enjoyed the prestige that it brought to him and to his family. He had a combustible and a prolific imagination which invested the temple with enchantment. It was a world of myriads of perfumes; the perfume of jasmine and orange blossoms mixed with incense and burning tapers. Some perfumes were faint and subtle, and others were heady and powerful. It was also a world of subdued and soothing music in which hymns were sung to the accompaniment of magic lyres. During this entire "service," Salman sat, lulled by music, and watching in fascination, the wild and erratic dance of the red, orange and turquoise flames racing out of the "eternal fire." It was a strange, unreal, astral world that he "inhabited" for many hours every day. The elements making up that world were the perfumes, the music, the "silent" and steady flames of the candles, and the hissing and crackling flames of the sacred fire.

* * * * *

For three years, Salman played priest in the fire-temple of Jiyye but then he began to lose interest in his work. It had become too monotonous and wearisome for him. The incantations of the priests were repetitious, dreary and empty of meaning. They were men of limited vision and limited knowledge - cagy ecclesiastics, with a stereotyped religion and crabbed minds - and they were too dogmatic, as he found out, even at that tender age. If he posed any creedal questions to them, they were, in most cases, unable to answer him; or, they spoke in a language of allusions, mystical parables, historical allegories and parallels. Salman, however, preferred direct answers. But instead of admitting their ignorance, they tried to dismiss his questions as impertinent, or they tried to browbeat him into silence. They were piteously parochial in outlook, and showed little interest in or awareness of the world beyond their homes and the temple.

21

Their homes and the temple were the two poles of their existence. And they were old men - some old enough to be his grandfathers. He had growing difficulty in establishing rapport with them - an early example of the generational conflict.

Salman vaguely felt that his soul thirsted for something else - something that was mysterious and elusive. He did not know what it was but whatever it was, he sensed that he could not find it in the cult of Zoroastrianism. He suddenly began to wish he could exchange his priesthood for a less pedestrian trade. He didn't want to spend the rest of his life vegetating as a priest in a fire-temple in a small, provincial town. His heart hungered for a more spacious and challenging existence than Jiyye could offer. His roving mind travelled in distant regions and mysterious realms. He longed to discover new horizons and to explore new worlds. He felt that his restless spirit was in chains but was making desperate efforts to break them, and to become free.

Salman knew that he would become free if he found the Ultimate Truth. But what was the Ultimate Truth, where was it, and how could he find it? These questions became an obsession for him.

In a sense, Salman's experience with the national church of Persia had been counter-productive. It had made him a "free-thinker" or rather a skeptic. He questioned its claims and its dogmas. But finding no satisfactory and convincing answers to his questions, he began to wonder if there didn't exist other categories of experience different from his own which might be the repository of the Ultimate Truth.

* * * * *

It appears that Salman's destiny, in response to his silent yearnings, was already at work to secure his "deliverance" from the constricting ambience of the fire-temple, and of Jiyye itself, though he could not read its "signals" at the time.

One day in spring (circa A.D. 586), Salman's father had some important business to attend to at one of his country-houses. But before he could go to the country, some merchants arrived in Jiyye from the ancient city of Balkh, bringing with them many rare and precious gifts from China for him. They were his guests, and to entertain them he had to stay in Jiyye itself. He, therefore, asked Salman to go in his stead, and briefed him on what he had to do at the country-house.

The following day was a Sunday. Salman rose long before the "false-dawn," got dressed, and left his home, riding his sleek, muscular and richly caparisoned horse, through the serpentine streets and sinuous lanes of Jiyye. Soon he was out of its walls.

When Salman had travelled a few miles from the city, he came upon a fork in the road, and standing upon the brow of an eminence, he paused for a few minutes to survey the surroundings and to determine the direction of his destination.

The light was now rapidly advancing from the east, and was tinting the landscape. Cherry trees were casting pink petals on the ground. The air had a sharp and a crisp tang to it, and wantonly mussed the mane of Salman's horse. Presently the sun rose. First a band of golden light above the horizon, and then the red disk appeared above the land. All around Salman, a maze of hills, rocks, cliffs, clusters of houses, groves of trees, fields, wild flowers, birds and squirrels, and butterflies and dragonflies, began to materialize like a world being born, or rather, being re-born. The day-break was, in fact, the daily miracle of the rebirth of the sun and the earth.

The world was settling into focus. Its new "dimensions" were peace, harmony, and solitude. The golden light of the new-born sun filled the space between heaven and earth. The landscape itself was highly photogenic but the sun, spiring upward through rays of saffron and orange into a point of white radiance, had added the touch of magic to it. Salman was held "captive" between a gilded sky and a gilded earth. That morning, in all its dewy and pristine freshness, had the impact of revelation upon him. He had not realized until then that a morning could be so beautiful. He, therefore, lingered a little longer, soaking in its ethereal beauty, serenity, glory and immaculacy.

Salman was still basking in the stream of the rays of the rising sun when a greystone edifice, partly veiled in golden mist, caught his eye. It was a newly built structure, and its style of architecture was different from the styles of architecture then in vogue in Persia. It was at some distance from the road, and Salman decided to find out what it was and to whom did it belong. He, therefore, went near it to take a closer look at it. The door of the edifice was open, and he heard some men singing in it. He thought that they were singing hymns.

Salman dismounted from his horse, tied it to a lamp-post and propelled by his curiosity, entered the building to investigate who were the singers and what were they singing.

Salman found himself in a hall of high walls. A choir was singing a hymn in a foreign language which he did not understand. The singers were all dressed in black tunics. Some of them were wearing white-pleated headdresses, the hair braided and coiled round upon the head. Too much penance and austerity, it was obvious, had made them lean and emaciated.

Salman was much astonished and intrigued by what he saw. However, he sat down quietly in the rear of the hall, and enjoyed the soothing music. When the service was over, one member of the congregation came to him, greeted him, and asked him who he was, and what was the purpose of his visit.

Salman told him who he was, and explained that he wished to know who they were, and what creed it was that they professed. He also asked his interlocutor if that hall was a temple, and if it was, why there was no fire in it.

The man held Salman by his hand and took him to the "high

priest," and said to him: "This young man is the son of the landlord of Jiyye. He wants to know who we are, and what we are doing here, and he is asking if this building is a temple.

The "high priest" welcomed Salman, and in answer to his questions, said:

(Priest): My son, we are Christians, and this building is a temple. We call it a church. We believe that God is one, and He is the Creator of the universe. We also believe that there will be a Day of Judgment. We know that there is such a thing as Salvation or Heaven, and there is such a thing as damnation or Hell, and we believe that the choice between the two is entirely ours.

Salman: But is there any God other than the god of Light, the god of Fire?

Priest: God is the Creator of Heaven and Earth. He is the Creator of Light and Fire. He is the Creator of all of us, and of all living things, and of all inanimate things. As for the fire in the temple or fire in the hearth, it is we who make it. We make it, and we put it out. Once it is put out, it becomes ashes. How can it be god?

Salman was plunged into deep thought. He felt that the words of the Christian priest were seared on his heart. Then another question arose in his mind, and he asked:

(Salman): Salvation and damnation; Heaven and hell! How do you know about them?

Priest: God sent His Apostles, Messengers and Prophets to this world, and they told us about them.

Salman: And who are these Apostles, Messengers and Prophets?

Priest: They are human and they are mortal like us. But God chose them and honored them, and inspired them with His message, and commanded them to deliver it to mankind, and to invite it toward Him. They preach His unity; they forbid idolatry, and they command everyone to do good deeds.

The priest then told Salman the story of the messengers of

God beginning with Adam. The last of them all, he said, was Christ, son of Virgin Mary - the Prophet of the Christians.

Salman felt as if the pious Christian priest had suddenly removed a veil from his eyes, and he could "see" new horizons which he did not see before. And he felt that his heart, "dark" until then, was flooded with a new and a powerful light. No doubt was left in his mind that this religion was better than the religion of the Zoroastrians. He, therefore, declared that he intended to become a Christian. He abjured his former religion. He proclaimed that God alone was all Power, and there was no other power, and that He was One and had no partners, and He was the Creator of everything. He further said that he believed that there would be a Day of Judgment and that Heaven and Hell exist.

Salman requested the high priest to initiate him into the new faith.

The priest formally initiated Salman into Christianity.

The Christians were happy that Salman had embraced Christianity. They congratulated him on his decision, and they welcomed him into the ranks of the faithful but their chief said to him:

(The Priest): I hope you will be steadfast in your new religion but I would advise you not to disclose it to your people. If you do, they may not like it. They will harass you and they might even persecute us.

Salman: But why my master? After all we are the rightly-guided ones, and they are the ones who have deviated from Truth.

Priest: Yes, that is true. But your people will not see it that way. They believe that they are the guardians of Truth, and that we are the ones who have gone astray. They will belittle us and our religion. And also, you should know that we fled from persecution in our own country. Now we do not want to do anything that might alarm your people, and make them our enemies.

Salman: Sir! Where are you from, and where was Christianity

born?
Priest: We came from Syria, and that's where our religion was
also born.

* * * * *

Salman was so deeply engrossed in his new discovery that he lost
all count of time. He even forgot the business for the execution
of which his father had sent him to his country-house. He spent
the whole day with his new Christian friends; posed many questions
to them, and did not stop questioning them until he had found
complete satisfaction on every point.

At midday, the Christians invited Salman to share their repast
of barley soup, rye bread, cheese, vegetables, eggs and fruit with
them which he did. He then visited their farm behind the church.
The farm was hedged by pickets of birch and cottonwood trees.
His friends told him that they grew most of their food at the farm
itself.

Salman had irrepressible curiosity. He requested the Christian
priests to show him their scriptures and other books. They were
only too willing to oblige, and led him into the church library
where they showed him the collection of parchment on which
their sacred lore was preserved. He took great pleasure in handling
the ancient manuscripts of the fathers of the Nestorian church,
and in admiring the ornamental writing on the scrolls. He regretted
his inability to read them but made up his mind to learn the
mysterious language and then to read them.

Toward late afternoon, there was another prayer-session in
the church which Salman attended. He even tried to sing the
hymns though not with much success. Christian prayer seemed
to him to be much more real and inspiring than the "Magian"
worship of the Persians. After the prayer, he returned to the
library to re-examine the manuscripts and the scrolls. He was

consumed by the desire to know what the fathers of the church had written in them.

The sun had already set when Salman was suddenly roused from his reverie. He realized that he had to return home immediately. He, therefore, thanked his Christian friends for the new light they had shown him, and thus had rescued him from error, and he also thanked them for their hospitality. He promised to return on the following day, and then rode out of the church precincts.

It was a sparkling clear but moonless night. Salman, therefore, had only the starlight to aid him in navigation. The air was sweet with briar roses and honeysuckle. On either side of the highway, the sinister shapes of trees, rocks and hills were etched against the horizons. From the horizons, he lifted his gaze toward a flamboyant heaven, and was thrilled to see the Milky Way arching across the sky, like a River of Sacred Light, flowing, as it were, from its "source" in Eternity to its "mouth" in Infinity. Spread on both "banks" of the River of Light, were myriads of stars, some glittering so vividly as to be dazzling; others dim like the flecks of a distant fire - barely visible. But they all shone with authority. They were there, it occurred to Salman, not to convince but only to express the glory of the Creator, to attest His Reality and Power, and to declare His Omnipresence.

Salman was overwhelmed by the measureless majesty of the starry heavens. He was alone and yet not alone. The stars were his companions. He was in the center of a silent and immense but not by any means, an empty and inanimate universe. The universe around him was sentient; it was throbbing with life and with mystery. The sky above him was vibrant and "alive." He felt he could almost take its "pulse" in his hand, and he could almost hear its "heartbeat."

Salman was lost in wonder. He was lost in contemplation of the incandescent heaven. Peace appeared to him to be a new entity that was almost "perceptible." And if he had known the Pythagoreans, he would have agreed with them that all heaven was Harmony. Occasionally, a star shot across the sky, and recollection came to him of the sparks and ripples of fire and the restless flames leaping and dancing in his fire-temple; but he knew that he was not going to enter it again. He had made up his mind to return to the church on the following day to see his Christian friends. But he was also eager to meet the merchants from Balkh. In anticipation of meeting them, he started framing questions in his mind on the people of China, their customs and their beliefs.

When Salman was late in coming home, his father became very anxious. Salman was his only child and in him he had invested all his hopes and dreams of the future. He sent his slaves and domestics all around town and to the country-house to find him, and to bring him home. They went but they could not find him anywhere. His father sat, hacked with nameless fears and dark forebodings, in the court of his palatial house, surrounded by his friends who were trying to comfort him and reassure him. Suddenly he (Salman) entered through the gate. His father threw his arms around him, smothered him with kisses and asked him where he had disappeared.

Salman: Father, I rode past a church of the Christians. I went inside it and I saw them praying. I liked their mode of worship, and I was with them all day long.

Father: My son, I hope that those people did not mislead you. Their religion is rank heresy. Your religion and the religion of your forefathers alone is the right one.

Salman: No father! It's not so. Their religion is better than ours. They worship One God, and we worship fire. Actually, we are the makers of that fire, and as soon as we stop feeding it, it dies and becomes ashes.

* * * * *

29

Salman's father was miffed by his reasoning but he was also silenced by its essential logic, and did not know what to say in reply to it. However, he was not convinced that Salman was right. He, therefore, first tried to dissuade him from adopting the new "heresy" but it did not work. He then thought that the argument of brute force might prove to be more effective to reconvert his "straggling" son to his ancestral faith, and said to him:

> "My son, I want you to swear that you have not changed and you will not change your religion. I also want you to swear that you will not see the Christians again. If you do not swear, I shall put you in chains, and you will spend your days in the dark and dank dungeons beneath our house until you come back to your senses." 'Salman refused to swear', and said:

Father, do what you like but I will follow the religion of Christ to which God in His mercy has guided me. As for you and your forefathers, all of you are in error.

Salman's father was thrown into a violent rage when he heard this comment on his religion by him. He ordered his slaves to take him (Salman) to the dungeons below the house, and to put him in chains.

Next day, Salman's father paid him a visit in his cell, and implored him to abandon Christianity, and to return to his former religion. When Salman refused to comply, his father sent his friends and the priests of the fire-temple to plead with him. But Salman ignored the pleas of them all, and refused even to discuss the subject with them.

Salman's father was not discouraged by these failures, and visited him every day for several weeks in the hope of talking him out of his "madness," but all his efforts were unavailing. At last, he was convinced that Salman had become an "apostate," and was "lost" beyond all hope of redemption. He had been very proud of him, and had often boasted among his compeers about his (Salman's) many accomplishments. But now he (Salman) had become not only a renegade, and had given up the prestigious and lucrative post at the fire-temple, but also had hurt his (the father's) pride by showing himself so "obstinate" in "sin and error." His pride was hurt and he decided to make Salman pay the penalty for his recalcitrance.

Salman was beaten and tortured, and was kept hungry and thirsty in his prison day after day but he showed no sign of yielding to pressure or to threats and to physical violence. He made it clear to his father that he was not going to worship the element of fire ever again or to abjure the new creed he had adopted.

In his solitary confinement, Salman began to wonder if the rest of his life would be spent as a prisoner. He recoiled in horror from the mere thought, and he began to see visions of regaining his freedom by making an attempt to escape from his home, and if possible, from Persia itself.

One of the servants of Salman's father was a young man called Mehran. He had reared Salman from his infancy, and he loved him like his own son. It grieved him to see Salman being held prisoner. He often came to see him and brought him news of the world outside. Salman also knew that he could trust Mehran, and asked him one day if he could put him in touch with the Christian priests who might assist him in escaping to Syria.

Mehran was only too glad to give this service to his young master. As he had expected, the Christian priests were very sad to know that Salman was being tortured for his conversion to the true faith. They asked Mehran to tell him to be patient, and to put his trust in God's mercy for his deliverance. They told

31

Mehran that they would alert him as soon as a caravan was ready, and would send Salman to Syria with it.

Salman, thereupon, braced himself for a long wait.

But not many days had passed when one night Mehran came to see Salman and informed him that a caravan of merchants and pilgrims, including some Christians, was ready to leave for Syria, and that the Christian priests had called him to their church on the following night.

Salman was very happy to learn that he was going to be free. He could not believe that he had such good fortune. However, it was still too early for him to rejoice in his freedom. He knew that he would be really free only when he would be beyond the reach of his father.

On the following night, Salman was too keyed up to sleep. Toward midnight, Mehran entered his cell, removed the shackles from his feet, gave him a new set of clothes to wear, and led him quietly out of the house when everyone was sound asleep.

Outside the house, a horse was awaiting Salman. In the saddlebag, Mehran had put coins of gold and silver and some other essentials that his young master would need during his long journey. Salman mounted the horse, took a last look at the house in which he was born and had grown up, thanked Mehran for his invaluable help, bade him a silent and tearful farewell, and rode out of Jiyye.

Upon arrival in the church, Salman noticed that the caravan was ready to march. He thanked his Christian friends for what they were doing for him. Their friendliness, courtesy and solicitude strangely counterpointed his own father's gruffness and tantrums. They told him that the caravan would take him to Damascus in Syria, and they gave him a letter for the chief monk of a monastry in that city. The monk, they further said, would arrange board and lodging for him in Damascus.

The priests also gave special instructions to the leader of the caravan regarding the welfare of Salman. He promised to do everything to make Salman's journey safe and comfortable for him.

The high priest then committed Salman to the protection of God.

The caravan left Jiyye the same night, and moving at a brisk pace, put considerable distance between itself and the city before daybreak.

Salman was never to return to Jiyye again.

* * * * *

Chapter III

The Years in the Wilderness

As the caravan traversed the vast expanses of Persia in its westward journey, the landscape kept changing until many days later, it left the Persian plateau behind it, and entered alluvial plains. One of the Christian travellers told Salman that they had crossed the boundaries of Persia, and that they were in another country - an alien country - not one subject to the laws of Persia. An alien country? Yes! And yet, to Salman it seemed more friendly than his own ancestral Persia. He now felt reassured that he would not be captured by his father's slaves, and he thanked God for rescuing him from prison, and from the brutality of his father.

During the long journey, Salman's caravan halted in many towns and villages either to sell and to buy merchandize, or to rest or to take fresh supplies. It also marched past many churches and monastries, and Salman saw devout men worshipping in them. Occasionally, he also worshipped with them. He could not help feeling pity for those people in his country who worshipped the element of fire, and he felt regret for all their lost effort in propitiating gods that didn't exist.

Nearly a month after its departure from Jiyye in Persia, the caravan arrived in the ancient city of Damascus. The leader of the caravan said to Salman: "This is Damascus - your destination. Live in it in peace and security." He congratulated him on

34

his success in escaping from Persia, and wished him well for his future. Salman thanked him and he thanked other members of the caravan who had helped him in any way during the journey, said farewell to each of them and parted company with them. Salman was happy to leave the heat and the dust of the desert behind him, and he was happy to be in Damascus. Damascus was an oasis of mellow tranquillity, rich in history and tradition, and it was a city of many churches and gardens. From an inn-keeper he obtained directions to go to the monastry in which he was going to live. The monastry was at the bank of a stream. Salman met its chief monk, and presented to him the letter from his Christian friends in Jiyye.

The chief monk welcomed Salman to Syria, treated him to monastic hospitality, and then lodged him in one of the cells of the ancient monastry.

Salman had come to the journey's end but quite frequently, the end of one journey is the beginning of another. Salman too had a new journey ahead of him but he knew that the new journey would be in the realm of spirit.

Salman peeked out of the window of his cell in the monastry at the new horizons in Syria, and he tried to look ahead into his own future. But one was as much "terra incognita" for him as the other.

For a long moment, Salman was lost in contemplation. In his new surroundings, he was an absolute stranger. He was tempted to go out and explore the area around the monastry. But after a month-long journey, he was exhausted, and his limbs needed rest. He, therefore, deferred exploration until the following morning. The anticipation of new experiences kept him awake for some more time but not for long, and soon he fell asleep.

* * * * *

Salman at this time was in the nineteenth year of his life. He was rangy and muscular, and had a powerful build. He was endowed with a highly retentive memory, and a most penetrating intelligence. He had a critical and an analytic mind that applied logic to every situation. In his physical characteristics and his mental attributes, he surpassed all the young men of his age and generation. Just as he was tall, broad and robust beyond his years, he was also wise, prudent and sagacious beyond his years and his experience. Early in life, he had cultivated a temperate personality. In Jiyye - his hometwon - he had riches, luxury, pleasure, and high status - all within grasp. But he spurned them all, and he did so notwithstanding his extreme youth. Instead of seeking power and pleasure, as other young men of his generation did, he made the pursuit of Knowledge and Truth the "vocation" of his life. He was the idealist par excellence.

* * * * *

After leaving Jiyye in Persia, Salman lived in four other cities. He lived for ten years in Damascus, and then during the next twenty years, he lived in Mosul, Nasibin and Ammuria. In each of these cities, he read, studied, observed, and he assimilated all the religious knowledge that was extant. He also spent much time in devotions in the hope of finding the gift of enlightenment and inner peace. But his religious experience during this period was almost entirely subjective. It arose out of and was identified by means of his awareness of his own mental states and psychological processes. There were times when his interior world became so vivid that he lost touch with the exterior world. This alarmed him. One question that arose persistently in his mind was if it was right to turn one's back upon the world and its problems, and to try to win felicity and inner peace for one's own self.

When Salman looked around himself, he found that tyranny and oppression were rampant, and everywhere the strong was exploiting the weak. He asked himself if his own inner peace would be real if he abandoned all that mass of suffering, toiling humanity to itself so he could win bliss and salvation for himself. In the beginning, Salman had no doubt that Truth and Salvation were to be found through the teachings of Christianity - through Nestorian Christianity which he had embraced. He, therefore, relentlessly sought truth and salvation in it. This quest led him to meet a multitude of Christian monks, priests, hermits, bishops and scholars, and he discussed many problems relating to religious experience with them. But most of them, he gathered, were interested only in personal salvation.

It is a commendable aim to try to obtain personal salvation, and Salman wanted his own salvation no less than anyone else. But he was not entirely convinced that there would be salvation for someone who had screened out the reality of God's religion in society by being oblivious of the sufferings of others. He knew that it was not possible for him to pursue religion entirely privately.

With the passage of time, the specter of doubt began to rear its head in Salman's thoughts. He felt that Truth - the Ultimate Truth - was still hidden from his sight, and this after an effort to find it that spanned more than a quarter of a century. But why? He often asked himself. He was happy that he had found Christianity but he knew that it had not slaked his thirst for the knowledge of Truth. Also, there were fundamental questions relating to the mystery of life and death, God's great design for the world, and the purpose behind it; the existence of evil and the morality principle; the beginnings and endings; the precise role of religion in man's life; the nature of the soul; the frontiers of knowledge; the limits of human experience; the paradoxes and contradictions of life; the ultimate criterion of the good and the right; the checkered destiny of man, and many others which it had been unable to answer.

Salman prayed, fasted, did penances, agonized, made resolutions and read the sacred lore of Christianity which was available to him in the churches and monastries of Syria, but the serenity, the vitality and the power which he sought, eluded him. He knew that in his quest he had been persistent and sincere and yet it had remained unproductive of any results.

Salman remembered that many years earlier when he was a young priest in the fire-temple of Jiyye, his questions had planted many reservations in his mind about Zoroastrianism. Those reservations had eventually impelled him to forsake Zoroastrianism and to adopt Christianity. But now similar reservations were being generated in his mind vis-a-vis Christianity which it seemed to him, lacked both reality and substance. Was his earlier experience going to repeat itself? He was afraid even to ask the question. No one expects historical parallels to fit exactly, but the similarity of reactions sometimes bewildered him.

After much reflection, analyses and soul-searching, over many years, Salman was convinced that Christianity and Judaism were not the perfect and the infallible codes for man's life. But if they were not, then which one was, he asked himself. After all, it was reasonable to assume that God must have revealed the perfect code of life to mankind. If so, where was it, and how could he find it, he wondered.

When Salman was tormented too much by these thoughts, and when he knew that he had come to an impasse, he turned to God, and prayed to Him to give him deliverance from doubt and skepticism, and to lead him to the destination which He had chosen for him. When he prayed, doubts ceased to assail him, and peace returned to his restless soul. Prayer restored to him the power to dream, to hope, to trust, to know and to act.

Salman had faith. He knew that God in His mercy would remove his distress, and would show him the light of guidance.

He was right. The light of guidance that he wished and hoped to see, was soon to appear on the horizon.

Chapter IV

Slavery

The last city in which Salman lived, was Ammuria - a city in the eastern part of Asia Minor - then a province of the Eastern Roman Empire or the Byzantine Empire. It was in Ammuria that he heard, for the first time, vague reports of the appearance, in Makkah in Arabia, of a new prophet. According to these reports, this new prophet forbade the worship of idols and images and preached the doctrine of the absolute sovereignty and Oneness of God.

Could this be the answer to his prayers, Salman asked himself. Was it possible, he wondered, that this new prophet had brought a new dispensation - the perfect, comprehensive and infallible dispensation for mankind? If he had, then he might be the man with definitive answers to all the fundamental questions relating to the destiny of man, he reasoned.

Salman tried to gather more information on the new prophet. Before anything else, he wanted to know his name. He met travellers coming from the south, posed questions to them, and learned from one of them that the name of the new prophet was Muhammed.

Then one more year passed, and all that Salman could learn in that year about the Arabian prophet, was that he considered himself to be the last messenger of God to mankind.

* * * *

It occurred to Salman that the Flame of Truth which he was seeking, might be the one burning in Makkah in Arabia. Suddenly

40

Makkah appeared to be beckoning to him to come. He had lived, he thought, long enough in Ammuria, and time had come for him to move to a new place. It was obvious to him that his penances, meditations, and investigations during the long years of his sojourn in Ammuria, had failed to yield any positive results as far as his quest for Truth was concerned. He, therefore, made up his mind to go to Makkah to meet the Arabian prophet as soon as his circumstances would allow, and to interrogate him personally on the problems which had been perplexing him.

Toward late summer in that year, some travellers arrived in Ammuria from the south. Salman's enquiries revealed that they came from a city called Yathrib in Arabia. Makkah, he learned from them, was farther south, at ten days' journey. These travellers, he gathered, were traders who bred pedigreed horses in Arabia, and sold them in the neighboring countries where they were highly prized for their beauty, strength and swiftness. They told him that after selling their horses, they would return to Damascus to make connection with a caravan that was being "assembled" there for the return journey to Yathrib.

It is possible that these travellers included some merchants from Makkah itself. Actually, most of the horse traders did not belong to Yathrib but came from surrounding areas. Yathrib was the point of "assembly" and departure of their caravans. Dr. Taha Hussain of Egypt, writes in his book, *Al-Wa'd al-Haqq* (=The Promise of Truth), published in Cairo (Egypt) in 1972: "The caravans of Makhzoom visited, sometimes Syria and sometimes Iraq; and sometimes they also visited *the lands beyond Syria and beyond Iraq*." (page 22).

The Makhzoom was one of the clans of the tribe of Quraysh in Makkah all of whom made their living by trading. The members of this clan, like those of others in Makkah, carried their cargo to the north or north-east every summer. Occasionally, they went "beyond Syria" and "beyond Iraq." The land beyond Syria was Asia Minor, and the land beyond Iraq was Persia. These merchants exchanged not only their goods but also important and interesting news with their customers, and probably, it was through them that people in eastern Asia Minor and western Persia heard about Muhammed, the new prophet and his work in Makkah.

Salman met the leader of these horse traders and requested him to allow him to travel with them to Damascus, and thence to Yathrib. In return for this favor, he offered to pay him his modest savings.

The leader of the horse traders agreed. Salman gave him whatever he had of his worldly possessions, and then set out in quest of the Way of Salvation and Truth which he hoped, the Arabian prophet would or might show him.

The journey was long and arduous. But Salman endured the travail with stoical courage. While other travellers rode their camels or horses, Salman walked, a feat of endurance that astonished them.

Sometimes the thirsty travellers requested Salman to bring water for them from the wells which he did, and he also fed and watered their camels and horses. In exchange for this service, they allowed him to ride their camels, part of the way, and he rode pillion with them. He thus "earned" his rest.

Two weeks after leaving Ammuria, Salman and the Arab horse dealers reached Damascus. They rested a few days in Damascus, and when their caravan was ready to march, they left for Yathrib with it.

Damascus made Salman nostalgic. He visited the monastry in which he had spent many years; and met the acquaintances who were still around. He also availed of the opportunity to earn some money by working as a laborer. With the money thus earned, he bought a few necessities such as food and clothing.

Four days later, the caravan entered Arabia proper. Though

Salman had not crossed any determinate boundaries, he could sense a change in the air. He had entered a new ambience. He could now observe, at first hand, the mode of life in the desert - the range-land of the nomad. He saw the nomads and their bedraggled encampments. He also saw the villages of the sedentary Arabs. In the desert all habitations of men were built of smacks of impermanence. At night, Salman sat with the nomads or the village folks around their camp-fires, and heard the long monologues of their story-tellers. Occasionally, a wild-eyed poet gave a recitation of his new lyrics, and thrilled the audience with his eloquence and his histrionics. Sometimes, a kahin (an Arab soothsayer) made an appearance at the camp-fire, and harangued the assembly with his "prognostications." The story-tellers, poets and the soothsayers, Salman noted, vied with each other to get public attention. These scenes struck him as being very weird; and the glow of fire, in the vast darkness of the desert, made them even weirder. But he was eager to learn everything about the new country. He, therefore, welcomed the opportunity to witness and to study the customs, habits, mores, traditions and folklore of his new "hosts" - the Arab people. He made up his mind that upon his arrival at his destination, he would soak himself in the culture of Arabia. The act of apprehending an alien culture is an intensely personal affair. For Salman, therefore, the journey through Arabia was as much a voyage of self-exploration, as it was a voyage of discovery.

* * * * *

The camp-fires were a refreshing diversion for Salman. They relieved the tedium and monotony of life in a world of sand. All he could see in any direction was sand - rolling, frothy and wavy sand - and it was forever in motion. Its motion was hypnotic; so also was the lulling, rhythmical symmetry of its surrealistic patterns. There were days when the only salients he could see on the sere and bleak earth, were the sand dunes or the line of mauve hills on the western horizon. But at other times, even the dunes and the hills disappeared, and the earth looked like an immense "pancake," with the immense vault of the sky, resting, as it were, on its rim. Salman was very much intrigued by the mirages of walled cities, gardens, lakes and streams but he soon learned to distrust them.

A frightful experience of the journey for Salman was a sandstorm. One afternoon, a violent wind came roaring from the hinterland in the east, and churned up the whole desert. It raised a cloud of fine dust and gritty sand which obliterated the sun, the horizons and the whole landscape. The grains of sand flew around like tiny but deadly "missiles" and they stung like sparks. In the featureless plain there was no protection anywhere against the fury of the escalating storm except behind the "rampart" of the crouching, snorting, protesting and disdainful camels.

Toward sunset, the violence of the storm reached a crescendo. Salman and the other travellers had swaddled themselves with clothes to keep the sand out of their eyes and ears, and pressed their faces against the sides of their camels who sat like "buffers" between them and the torrent of sand. Two hours after the sunset, the storm at last began to deescalate, and two more hours passed before it appeared to have spent its force.

Men and camels then dug themselves out of the deep sand-drifts. They looked less like men and camels and more like phantoms of the desert. Salman had feared that the sand might bury the whole caravan. He thanked God Who had saved their lives, and he prayed that he would never see such turbulence again.

* * * * *

44

The heat in the desert was infernal, and the thirst of the travellers was insatiable. The light and the heat of the sun bounced back from the shimmering grains of torrid sand and made their eyes smart. But they were veterans of travel in the desert, and they understood its variable, unpredictable and capricious moods. Salman, however, had yet to learn how to come to terms with his new environment. And since he had to walk more often than anyone else in the caravan, his feet were blistered and bruised and they bled. But neither the difficult terrain nor the inclemency of the elements nor his own painful feet, could daunt him. The glimmer of hope - faint but alive - of finding the Light of Truth in Makkah, propelled him, relentlessly and inexorably, and he forged ahead, without a gripe ever, toward his distant destination.

In summer months, travel in the Arabian desert during the day could become extremely exhausting, both for the riders and their mounts. Most caravans, therefore, travelled at night and rested during the day. The temperature fell after sunset, and the nights became cool and balmy. The desert, omnipotent, forbidding and menacing during the day, appeared to shed its "shell" of hostility, and to become "friendly" at night.

Very frequently, a singer also accompanied a caravan. The leader of Salman's caravan had brought a young and a gifted singer with him. He held the reins of the leading camel in his hand, and walked ahead of him, singing *hudi* - a love song of the desert - in Arabic.

The singer sang *hudi* in a rich and vibrant voice, and the camels fell in step with its plangent rhythms.

On moonlit nights, the desert acquired an uncanny quality. The hudi-singer serenaded the full-moòn with an ardor, an abandon and a gusto that seemed to transform the "soul" of the desert into a dancing flame. Perhaps he believed that he had, not only a terrestrial audience in the caravan of travellers, but also, a celestial audience in the caravan of the stars. His sonorous voice pierced the silence of the desert, and the moon - that "leader" of the caravan of the stars - itself, it seemed, was "carried away" by its wanton lilts.

Salman did not understand Arabic at this time but he wished that the hudi-singer would go on singing forever. He wished that the cool, tranquil and soothing nights would spin themselves into eternity. He dreaded the cruel days. All day long, he was haunted by the melody of the *hudi*, sung in the vast theater of the silent desert.

Occasionally, Salman saw caravans coming out of the hinterland of the desert in the south, and going toward Syria in the north. One of the most unforgettable sights that he ever saw, was the long train of camels silhouetted against a sunset sky. Sometimes, there were as many as three hundred camels in a train, and their line extended from horizon to horizon. Tiny bells suspended at the ankles of the camels, tinkled as they planted each foot on the ground, and the synchronized rhythm of the rise and fall of their feet at each step, produced the effect of a "carillon" - a carillon in the desolate desert. If Salman was sleeping, he woke up, and if he was working at something, he stopped - to hear the impromptu music. He beheld in fascination, the camels as they ambled past his caravan, until they vanished over the skyline or were engulfed in darkness; and he delighted in the music of the bells until it faded out in the distance.

The caravans appeared mysteriously, and then disappeared just as mysteriously, leaving only footprints of the camels on the sand. The echo of the receding "carillon" lingered in the desert air, and in Salman's ears, long after the passing of the caravans themselves.

A few days later, Salman's caravan arrived in the oasis of Wadi-ul-Qura in the Hijaz, and the leader of the caravan announ-

46

ced that they would halt there for three days and three nights. He ordered the travellers to unload the camels, to unpack their baggage, to let the animals rest, to replenish their stocks of food and water, and to take fodder for the animals before resuming journey to Yathrib itself.

Salman welcomed the chance to rest his aching limbs, to soothe his stinging eyes, to dress his bleeding feet, and to loll in the shade of the trees growing around a spring. This to him was the ultimate in luxury.

Salman luxuriated in cool and fresh water for three days. The water acted like a tonic upon his spirits, and a balm upon his weary limbs, and he felt limber and reinvigorated once again.

In Wadi-ul-Qura, Salman also made plans for travelling from Yathrib to Makkah. He consulted some other travellers in this regard, and they explained to him how he could make connection with another caravan travelling south from Yathrib to Makkah and to Yemen.

* * * * *

Salman carefully made plans for the last leg of his journey from Yathrib to Makkah. What he did not know at this time was that bitter disappointment was lying in wait for him "just around the corner." At the end of the period of rest and recuperation, bad luck was going to spring a most cruel surprise upon him.

The caravan rested for three days and three nights, and was then ready to travel again. But just before its departure, when the merchants were still giving finishing touches to their transactions, one of them conceived a wanton and a diabolical thought. Addressing his companions, he said;

> "There are many Jews in Wadi-ul-Qura. Let us tell them that this stranger (Salman) who came with us

from Ammuria, is our slave, and that we wish to sell him. His sale will fetch a high price considering that he has such a powerful physique. Since he is alone, and is unknown to everyone here, he will not be able to disprove what we say, and then we can all share the price that his buyer will pay us."

These merchants were unequalled anywhere for their cussedness, cynicism, and their lust for money, and they could not resist the temptation to make extra "profit" in this deal of infamy. Therefore, with the connivance, if not the collusion, of the leader of the caravan, they offered Salman for sale to the highest bidder among the Jews. Salman protested that he was not a slave, and could not be sold or bought but he could not produce any "witnesses" who would vouch that he was a free man. He was made a prisoner by his Jewish master, and the caravan left for its destination without him.

Within moments. Salman's estate had changed from one of freedom and honor to that of slavery and indignity. He was utterly heart-broken at this reversal of fortune. Suddenly, his life had become anchorless, and void of meaning and direction. Instead of reaching Makkah or Yathrib, he had run into a dead end, and he was at a loss to know how to find a resolution to the problem.

When the initial shock had passed, Salman took stock of the situation. It was too bad. It was utterly hopeless, and he realized that he was utterly helpless. But he also realized that he could not mull over his misfortune for long nor could he give up the struggle, and that he had to make the best of the circumstances. His faith in God's mercy alone sustained him in a situation which was comparable to something like a shipwreck.

In this painful moment, Salman might have identified himself with Prophet Joseph whose story was familiar to him. Joseph was a bright, promising and handsome young man. He was the beloved of his father, Prophet Jacob; and was himself chosen by God for prophethood. But his jealous half-brothers tried to block him from fulfilling his great destiny, and sold him into slavery.

Salman could take comfort from Joseph's story. Both of them were betrayed - Salman by his fellow-travellers, and Joseph by his half-brothers. But after many ups and downs in life, freedom was restored to Joseph, and he was elevated to the high rank of prophet.

It occurred to Salman that his own encounter with bad luck was perhaps a test for him, and if it was, then he ought not to flunk in it. He remembered that, many years, earlier, God had given him deliverance from prison and torture in his hometown. He, therefore, turned, once again, toward the same source of mercy, bounty and succor to give him deliverance from slavery also.

Salman's master put him to hard labor. Salman hated his work but he did whatever his master ordered him to do, and he tried to do it to the best of his (the master's) satisfaction. His work, whatever it was, could not be faulted for its quality.

Salman attracted much attention in Wadi-ul-Qura. His massive chest, gigantic stature and powerful limbs made him a very conspicuous figure, and many people, especially the farmers, showed an interest in buying him. But his master considered him a valuable asset, and turned down many an attractive offer.

One of the bidders, however, was a cousin of Salman's master. He lived in Yathrib and visited Wadi-ul-Qura from time to time on business. He became so insistent on buying Salman that his (Salman's) master agreed to sell him.

Salman's new master did not tarry long in Wadi-ul-Qura and took him to Yathrib where he put him to work in one of the oases.

Before long, in Yathrib also, a competition began among the Jews to buy Salman. His master did not want to sell him but he found one of the offers so attractive that he accepted it, and sold him. The new master sold him again. Thus he passed through many hands. Eventually, a rich Jew - one Uthman bin Ashhel - bought him. Uthman bin Ashhel was going to be Salman's last master. He refused to sell Salman to anyone at any price.

Uthman and the other Jews had never seen a slave like Salman. They noted that he didn't talk much but whenever he did, he spoke words of profound wisdom. His judgment, they noted, was like the judgment of Solomon himself. His master benefitted, not only from his work but also from his advice and his opinions which he sought from him quite frequently. But he was a vicious and a brutal taskmaster, and made Salman work almost non-stop.

Salman's work was difficult and laborious but he did not allow his adverse circumstances to extinguish the flame that the hope of meeting Muhammed had kindled in his breast. The hope of meeting Muhammed revived him each day. There was magic in the name of Muhammed that never failed to work. Whenever Salman had a rough day, he reminded himself that he had a "rendez-vous" with Muhammed, and he bounced back.

The hope of meeting Muhammed - his unseen beloved - some day - impelled Salman to learn his (Muhammed's) language - Arabic. Within an year or two of his arrival in Yathrib, Salman had taught himself Arabic, and he could speak it with perfect command, both of grammar and of vocabulary. He also taught himself "basketry" in such "spare moments" as he could find, and showed himself very skilful at it.

It must not be assumed that Salman had abundant leisure, and that he could apply himself to the study of languages, and he could acquire new skills as a craftsman. No. It was not so. His master allowed him no rest much less any leisure. But Salman was endowed with such exceptional talents that he could almost effortlessly learn anything and everything. Notwithstanding the many handicaps that his status as a slave imposed upon him, he seized every opportunity and every moment to learn something new.

As an observer also, Salman was highly gifted; and he was a perspicacious analyst of human nature and character. He despised the Jews for their coarseness, their lust, their perversity, their conceitedness, their sickening hypocrisy, their presumptuousness, their raw, grasping materialism, their obsession with money, and their readiness to acquire it by fair means or foul. The more he knew them, the more he was repelled by them.

The other ethnic group in Yathrib was made up of two Arab tribes called Aus and Khazraj. Salman had an opportunity of observing them also, and he found them hardly any better, if not worse, than the Jews. He was unable to conceal his contempt for them. They worshipped crude idols of stone and wood. They were ignorant and superstitious. They were arrogant and vindictive. They could fight against and kill each other for the most trivial of causes. They lived and they died in moral squalor and spiritual turpitude. They were reckless, shiftless and intemperate. Drunkenness was only one out of many of their vices. And they were forever burdened with debts to the Jews.

Such was the environment in which Salman found himself after losing his freedom. It reeked with foulness. He turned his eyes toward heaven, and prayed to God to send His Messenger to change it. Or, if God had already sent him, then he prayed to Him to lead him (Salman) to a meeting with him (with God's messenger). In prayer alone, Salman could find comfort and escape from the stifling and soul-strangling environment.

What Salman did not know at this moment, was that his prayer had already been heard in Heaven. God has His own mysterious ways of answering the prayers of His loving slaves.

* * * * *

51

Unknown to Salman, momentous events were taking place in Arabia. Muhammed Mustafa (may God bless him and his Ahlel-Bayt) had appeared in Makkah many years earlier. He had proclaimed his mission as the Last Messenger of God to mankind; and he had sent his uncle, Mas'ab ibn Umayr, to Yathrib, to propagate the new faith which was called Islam. Many leading figures of the Aus and Khazraj - the two Arab tribes of Yathrib - had accepted Islam, and they had invited Muhammed Mustafa to their city as their guest. The latter had accepted their invitation, and had in fact migrated to Yathrib. But Salman didn't know anything about these events.

Uthman bin Ashhel had many thousands of trees of date fruit. In the harvesting season, Salman had to take a huge bag or a basket, and he had to climb one of them. When he reached the top, he picked the fruit, filled the basket with it, and then came down to the ground, only to take an empty basket and climb up another tree. His master sat below in the shade of the trees gorging himself upon the succulent fruit that he (Salman) had plucked from the crown of the trees.

One morning, Salman was awaiting daybreak to begin his work. He sat under a tree, reflecting on his past and present, and wondering what could happen in the future that might bring his privation and drudgery to an end, and restore his freedom to him. For a few moments, he fancied himself a free man once again, and he almost got "lost in the clouds." But suddenly, he was jerked out of his dreamworld by the bark of his master who had materialized out of the darkness. He ordered him to begin his work even if it was still dark. Thereupon, Salman began the first of his endless and countless ascents and descents up and down the date-palms.

When the sun climbed up toward the zenith, the sky turned into a disc of fire that spewed flames onto the earth. At that moment, he (the sun) appeared to be the only "absolute" between sky and earth. Climbing a tree at mid-day was like crawling into a furnace. Salman went up the trees many times and returned with many basketfuls of date fruit, utterly frazzled out, but his master allowed him no rest beyond a pause long enough for him to drink some water. Since Salman was highly conscientious, he did not complain of his exhaustion, and pushed himself to the limits of endurance.

On the ground, Salman had other duties. He had to remove the stones from the fruit; he had to pack it and store it or he had to load it on camels. He had to draw water from the wells and to irrigate the fields, and he had to pull out the weeds.

Such exacting work drained all the blood and energy out of Salman but he was enabled to survive it day after day by the power of Faith. Whenever his spirits flagged, he turned to the unique, vital and transcendent power of prayer, and found cheer and comfort in it. In all his pains and pangs, he looked toward Heaven for strength, and it came to him. His prayer sprang from his conviction that he was not subject to brute force but was governed and sustained by the Law and Love of God.

There were times when the burden did seem to Salman to be unbearable, and he was tempted to be bitter. But, instead, he went into the silent sanctuary of his soul, and prayed to God, and came out sweetened, revived and reinforced. He had in his own heart that spring of renewal, which was made perennial by the power of prayer.

Prayer was an integral part of each day of Salman's life. It brought a sense of God's nearness to him. He also held the power of prayer like a shield against other people's wantonness. His prayers were deep and conscientious protests of Truth reaching the Gates of Divine Justice, Forgiveness and Redemption. No matter how brutal and inhuman the conditions under which he had to live and work, his rocklike faith in God's boundless mercy remained unshaken; he counted upon it to free him from captivity of every kind, and he never surrendered to despair.

The darkest hours of the night, it is said, are nearest to the dawn. The dark hours of the night for Salman the Persian also could not last forever. Slavery had been a very long and dark night for him. Even so, it was inevitable that its darkness would be routed by a glorious and a beautiful dawn.

* * * * *

One morning when Salman began his descent from the top of a tree, he noticed that his master, who sat at its foot, was engaged in talking with a stranger. He was still some ten feet above the ground when he heard the stranger say with considerable animation:

> "May God curse these Aus and Khazraj. They have taken the oath of loyalty to a man who came from Makkah, and who claims that he is a messenger of God."

A tremor of excitement ran down the powerful frame of Salman when he heard these words. They in fact threw him in such an agitation that he feared he might fall from the trunk of the tree on top of his master. But by a tremendous effort of will, he managed to control the tumult surging in him. He came to the ground, and asked the stranger:

> "Sir, who is this man you are talking about? What is his name and where is he now?"

Before the stranger could say anything, Salman's master rose from the ground, beside himself with rage at this intrusion. He struck Salman in his face with full force, and snapped:

> "Not your business. Don't meddle in these affairs. You were born only to be a slave, and your job is only to obey my orders. Now return to your work."

The stranger also chimed in with his remarks:

"You dare too much. These matters are far too important for someone like you to be concerned with. You ought to be content with what you have been ordered to do, and to do it well."

Salman was neither shocked nor surprised at his master's attitude. His master was a man who was utterly alienated from God. In sheer conceit, sordidness and depravity, few could match and none could surpass him. Salman hardly expected any different treatment. He, therefore, picked up an empty basket and braced himself to climb yet another tree. But suddenly he stopped. His attention was caught by a question that his master posed to the stranger.

The news of the events taking place in Yathrib was so important that Salman's master forgot him for the moment, and became engrossed in talking with his guest. Salman, therefore, decided to take advantage of his master's temporary absorption, and quietly occupied himself in removing stones from fresh dates. It was something he could do without attracting the unwelcome attentions of his master or of his guest, and this is what he heard:

Uthman bin Ashhel: Is it true what you have told me just now?

The stranger: Oh yes, it is absolutely true, and there is no doubt about it.

Uthman bin Ashhel: What is the name of this man from Makkah? What kind of messenger of God is he, and what does he want to do in Yathrib?

The stranger: His name is Muhammed ibn Abdullah. He is so presumptuous that he claims to be in the same line as our great prophets - Abraham, Isaac, Jacob, Joseph, Moses, David and Solomon. He further says that he is the last of the messengers of God, and that God will not send any other of His messengers to this world. An Aussite friend of mine told me that he (Muhammed) does not accept sadaqa (=charity), and says that it is unlawful for him and for members of his family. When he claimed that

55

God had sent him as His last messenger to mankind, the people of Makkah tried to kill him or to capture him. They placed a price on his head but he succeeded in escaping from there. Now he wants to live in Yathrib. The Aus and the Khazraj believe that he is the prophet God has sent to guide them, and to lead them out of error and sin. Many of them have already given him their pledge of loyalty as I said before, and they have also given him a pledge that they would protect him from his enemies.

Uthman bin Ashhel: Have all the Aussites and Khazrajites given him their pledge of loyalty?

The stranger: Yes.

Uthman bin Ashhel: If Aus and Khazraj have united, then it could mean trouble for us. They might make it impossible for us to live in Yathrib.

Uthman then posed another question.

Uthman: Tell me, my cousin, do you think that this man from Makkah is the same prophet whose advent has been foretold in our books?

The stranger: I do not know; but the Arabs say that he has all the signs of the prophets in him.

Uthman: Are our people going to follow him and believe in him?

The stranger: Heaven forbid that our people should ever follow a prophet who is not an Israelite. And is it at all imaginable for us to follow a prophet who is illiterate? This man is an Arab of the tribe of Quraysh of Makkah, and he is illiterate.

Uthman: If that is so, then what is going to be our attitude toward him?

The stranger: We have to open a war of nerves against him. We should rouse all the Arab tribes against him, and we should do everything we can to make his stay in Yathrib impossible so that he will leave it and go elsewhere.

Uthman: May God bless you, my cousin. You have spoken the words of wisdom. Our people must act upon your advice, and that is the only way to solve this problem.

* * * * *

Salman had heard every word that was exchanged between his master and his guest. Those words kept ringing in his ears like dulcet music. He had spent years of agony in the hope that he would, some day, hear those words, or words of the same import, and he had heard them at last. Could he believe it that Muhammed, the Messenger of God, was physically present in Yathrib, in the same city as he (Salman) was? Wasn't the news too good to be true? He dared not answer this question. But his morale was restored by the mere knowledge that he and Muhammed had become "neighbors," and he forgot the stress and distress of slavery.

Salman was unable to sleep that night. One question that kept spinning him in his bed was: "Now that Muhammed, the object of my quest, is in Yathrib, how soon can I see him with my own eyes?"

And as on so many occasions in the past, Salman relied, confidently and consistently, upon God's mercy to send him an answer to his unspoken question.

Chapter V

Salman's Meeting with Muhammed Mustafa (S) and his Induction into Islam.

The answer to Salman's question came sooner than he had expected it to come.

One evening Uthman bin Ashhel was away from the oasis on some business, and Salman availed of the opportunity to realize his wish. He put the ripe and fresh dates which he had earned that day as his wages, in a bag, and went into the city to find Muhammed (may God bless him and his family), and to have audience with him.

Muhammed Mustafa was living, at this time, in the house of Hadhret Abu Ayub Ansari (may God be pleased with him), as his guest. Each step that Salman took toward his destination, heightened his anticipation.

And then the great moment came. Salman the Persian was escorted into the presence of Muhammed Mustafa, the beloved of God, and his (Salman's) own unseen beloved. His heart was bounding inside his ribs like a bird fluttering in a cage but he was making a supreme effort to steady himself. Suddenly, he was arrested in mid-motion by the vision framed in the arch.

Muhammed Mustafa (may God bless him and his family) was seated in the reception room of the house. A few companions sat in front of him. Salman's first glance fell upon his face, and all at once he felt himself dazzled by a thousand sparkling lights. He heard himself saying quietly:

"By God, this cannot be the face of a man who has

ever told a lie. If there is any face that can be the face of a messenger of God, that is the face of this man."

For Salman, that face - the face of Muhammed - was like a sunburst in the dark!

Salman paused for a few moments at the threshold of the house to let the image of Muhammed Mustafa (may Allah bless him and his family) impress itself upon his soul, heart and mind, and it did.

Salman was then formally presented to the Messenger of God who welcomed him with a beatific smile, and signalled him to sit down in front of him.

After the exchange of preliminary greetings, Salman stated the purpose of his visit.

Muhammed Mustafa told Salman that the message that he had brought, was called Islam, and he explained its meaning to him as total surrender of man, without reservation, to the Will and pleasure of Allah. Salman could not wait long enough and begged Muhammed Mustafa to admit him to the company of those slaves of Allah who surrender themselves to His Will and His pleasure.

Muhammed Mustafa, the Messenger of Allah (may Allah bless him and his family), thereupon, inducted Salman the Persian into Islam. The first requirement for Salman in this induction , was to believe that God was One and had no partners or associates, and that Muhammed was His Messenger. The doctrine of the Oneness of God is called Tauheed, and it is the axis of Islam. The mission of Muhammed as God's last messenger to mankind is called Risalet. The second requirement for Salman was to declare his faith in Tauheed and in Risalet.

Salman complied with these requirements. He was now a Muslim (=one who submits to the Will of Allah); and a Momin

59

(=a true believer). Islam is the combination of Faith and a set of duties. Foremost among the duties of a Muslim is Salat or the five daily canonical prayers, viz., Fajr, Zuhr, Asr, Maghrib and Isha. But no one may say a prayer without purifying oneself. Muhammed Mustafa, the Messenger of Allah, instructed Salman into the manner of taking ablutions for personal purification, and into the manner of offering the canonical prayers.

Salman had been enlisted into the service of Allah by His Own Messenger - Muhammed Mustafa - an honor and a distinction he was to remain proud of all his life. At the same time, he was also admitted into the ranks of his (Muhammed's) friends.

* * * * *

The face is generally the first thing one notices when one meets or sees someone else. Judgments are often drawn from a person's face. Salman had never seen the face of Muhammed. But how he responded to Muhammed when he saw his face! The face - the countenance or character - of Muhammed was reassuring to Salman. Delineated in that face he could read Beauty, Purity, Sinlessness, Sincerity and Truth.

Maulana Abul Kalam Azad, one of the principal architects of India's independence, and independent India's first Minister of Education, writes in his biography of the Prophet of Islam, called *Rasul-e-Rahmet* (=Messenger of Mercy), published in Lahore, Pakistan (1970) as follows:

> "When Salman el-Farsi came into the presence of the Messenger of Allah, he exclaimed: 'By God! This is not the face of a man who has ever told a lie in his life.' One look at the face of Muhammed was enough to convince him that he (Muhammed) was, without a doubt, the Messenger of Allah. With love, zeal and conviction, he declared that God was One, and

Muhammed was His Slave and His Messenger."

* * * * *

For Salman, a life-long quest had at last come to an end with a victorious note of the superseding, intervening power of God. His whole existence had been redeemed and reoriented.

Salman thanked Allah in silence for bestowing the blessing of Islam upon him - His humble slave. The experience for him was too profound and too moving to find expression in words:

THOSE WHOM GOD (IN HIS PLAN) WILLETH TO GUIDE, - HE OPENETH THEIR BREAST TO ISLAM.
(Quran Majid. Chapter 6; verse 125)

All the companions and friends of Muhammed Mustafa who were present at the occasion, congratulated Salman for receiving the blessing of Islam - the greatest of all the blessings of Allah.

* * * * *

It was not only Salman who was convinced, just by taking one look at the face of Muhammed that he was a true Messenger of God; the latter was also convinced, just by taking one look at his (Salman's) face that he (Muhammed) had found, in him, a true believer and a sincere friend. There was character in that face, steady eyes, a firm mouth, and an intelligent forehead. "Personal chemistry" was at work on both sides. It was a case of "love at first sight" between Muhammed Mustafa and Salman el-Farsi.

The first meeting of Muhammed Mustafa, the Messenger of Allah, and Salman the Persian - the two slaves, the two friends and the two lovers of Allah - must have been one of the most touching, most memorable and most dramatic scenes in the epic of Islam.

* * * * *

After his "induction" into Islam, Salman presented the dates to Muhammed Mustafa, and said: "O Messenger of Allah! I can see some poor people here. Some of them may be hungry. I have brought these dates as my *sadaqa* (=charity). Please ask them to eat it."

Muhammed Mustafa thanked Salman for the dates and then invited his companions to eat them. Salman noted that he himself did not touch them.

* * * * *

Salman found Muhammed Mustafa so charismatic that he did not want to part company with him even for a moment. He felt that his soul, his heart and his mind were all being taken captive - by Muhammed - and that he had neither the strength nor the will to resist him. He had never had such an experience before.

That night Salman hardly touched the earth as he walked toward his home in the oasis. So buoyed up was he in soul and body. Muhammed had set him free from all anxieties, fears, doubts and frustrations. He felt as free as a bird.

Four weeks later, Salman was able to pay another visit to the Prophet. Once again he brought fresh dates - his wages - with him; but this time not as sadaqa (charity) but as a present for the Prophet himself. The latter accepted the present, thanked Salman for it, partook of some dates from it, and distributed the rest among his companions.

* * * * *

Induction into Islam was an appropriate occasion for change of Salman's name. His Persian name was Rozeba. Muhammed Mustafa, the Messenger of Allah, changed it to Salman. Salman loved his new name; he forgot his Persian name, and he is known to history only by his Islamic name.

Then Muhammed Mustafa (may Allah bless him and his family) read, for Salman's edification, some passages from Quran Majid - the Book revealed to him by Heaven - and he was carried away by its magisterial cadences. He had never before in his life, heard any composition so sublime. Those words which he heard, were "incandescent," and he sensed that they could not have been put together anywhere but in Heaven itself. They reached into his bosom, and plucked his heart out of it.

Muhammed Mustafa, the Messenger of Allah, had thus introduced Quran to Salman. The two of them - Quran and Salman - immediately struck up a "partnership" that became and remained indissoluble for all time. The exordium to the Book of Allah, given by Allah's Own Messenger, was an ecstatic experience for Salman. He knew that he had been conquered. The liberating, benevolent and triumphant power of the Book of Allah had conquered him. He had not asked any questions as was his habit, but he knew that the conquest was irreversible.

Salman the Persian had reached the high point of his life. All his life he had sought an idyll, and at length, he had captured it. He had trusted God to reveal to him the Ultimate and the Eternal Truths, and He had, in response to his prayer, revealed them to him - through Muhammed - in His Book, Quran Majid!

Salman also realized that Quran was a Book that demanded commitment from him. He, therefore, resolved that he would make, the rest of his life, an expression of his commitment to the ideals of that Book.

* * * * *

Salman came to see the Messenger of Allah as often as he could, and each time, he brought, either a present for him or sadaqa (charity) for his companions. He brought only what he had earned as his wages.

It was inevitable that Salman would arouse the curiosity of the

Muslims who had seen him; just as earlier, he had, that of the Jews. He was a commanding and a compelling figure. He spoke eloquent but heavily accented Arabic. But more than his stature and his rugged and heavy-duty constitution or his speech, it was the purity of his perception of Allah, and his love for Muhammed Mustafa, that caught attention. That love had a touching quality to it; it was transcendental love. But he was still a figure of mystery, and no one at the court of Muhammed Mustafa knew who he was and how he came to Yathrib but everyone was eager to know. Eventually, Muhammed Mustafa (may Allah bless him and his Ahlel-Bayt) himself asked him to tell the story of his life.

Salman said: "O Messenger of Allah! I have spent more than thirty-five years of my life searching for the Light of Truth, and I have spent more than five years searching for you. Praise be to Allah that I found you at last; and through you, I found the object of my long quest - Truth. I thank Allah for His mercy that He made my quest fruitful." Salman then recounted the saga of his life.

Muhammed Mustafa, the Messenger of Allah, and his companions heard Salman's story in rapt fascination. They were deeply moved, and they were amazed at his persistence and his perseverance in seeking, and at his success in eventually finding, the Messenger and the Message of Allah.

Muhammed Mustafa (may Allah bless him and his Ahlel-Bayt) embraced Salman, kissed him on his forehead, rubbed his hand over his (Salman's) face, and over his heart; prayed for him, and invoked Allah's mercy and His blessings upon him. It was a poignant moment in the life of both of them.

And it was a moment so rich in drama that it "jelled" in the hearts and minds of Salman and all the companions of the Prophet of Islam who were present at the occasion, and had heard his (Salman's) story. It was an unforgettable moment for them all.

Salman the Persian was the first "conquest" of Islam from Christianity. He was, therefore, the forerunner of all those men and women who at one time were Christians but latter became Muslims. His rebellion against tradition, as sanctified in Persia by the authority of the "national" (Zoroastrian) church, and in Syria by the authority of entrenched Christianity, is the backdrop of his conversion to Islam. His conversion is also a gripping study of a "pilgrim's" progress as he moved from the non-revealed religion of Zoroastrianism in Persia to the inspired religion of Christianity in Syria to the revealed religion of Islam in Arabia.

* * * * *

Salman was literally drawn from Ammuria in Asia Minor to Yathrib in Arabia by the light of the "lamp" of the prophethood of Muhammed Mustafa, just as a moth is drawn to a flame in a glass. For years, he had wandered from city to city in quest of Truth, and had failed to find it anywhere. At length a light beckoned to him from Yathrib. He went there and found the "Light" of Muhammed flickering like a flame on the vast breast of the desert, in the darkness of the Arabian paganism. But he also noticed that the hurricane of paganism threatened to extinguish the "flame," and he made himself a "shield" for it. From that moment, his life was consecrated to the service of Islam and of its Prophet, Muhammed Mustafa (may Allah bless him and his Ahlel-Bayt).

Salman reoriented his life toward God. Islam changed his relationship with God. He now saw that relationship in a new perspective. He realized that without God's mercy there could be no happiness or peace or success for him, and he knew that His grace alone could brighten the darkness of his life, and lift him out of his joyless and meaningless living, and it did. God's boundless bounty encircled him and his all.

AND THOSE WHO STRIVE IN OUR (CAUSE),
WE WILL CERTAINLY GUIDE THEM TO OUR PATHS:
FOR VERILY, GOD IS WITH THOSE WHO DO RIGHT.
                                    (Quran Majid. Chapter 29; verse 69)

For Salman, Islam was a Multiple Blessing. Not only it had liberated him from all kinds of false worship; not only it had brought to an end his "maverick" existence; and not only it had given him a focus in life; but also, it had won for him the friendship of God's Own Beloved - Muhammed Mustafa. His heart was brimming with gratitude. He had no doubt that Allah had picked him out, expressly, so he could become the recipient of the blessing of Islam. He, therefore, lifted his eyes and his hands toward Heaven in thanksgiving to Him.

THEN THOSE WHO BELIEVE IN GOD, AND
HOLD FAST TO HIM, - SOON WILL HE
ADMIT THEM TŎ MERCY AND GRACE FROM
HIMSELF AND GUIDE THEM TO HIMSELF BY
A STRAIGHT WAY.
                                    (Quran Majid. Chapter 4; verse 175)

* * * * *

If ever there was an "El Dorado" of Faith and Love for anyone, it was Yathrib for Salman. He discovered the El Dorado of Faith and Love aided directly in that discovery by the Mercy and Grace of Allah!

* * * * *

(Note: One of the companions who heard the story of Salman, was Abdullah ibn Abbas. He was the first cousin of the Prophet and Ali ibn Abi Talib. The historians have quoted him for most of the details of the story of the life of Salman until the time he became a Muslim.)

* * * * *

A few months after the acceptance of Islam by Salman, the name "Yathrib" fell into disuse, and a new name - *Medinat-un-Nabi* - "The City of the Prophet," was chosen for it. But in due course, it came to be known simply as "Medina" - the City.

Medina or "the City" which, after the migration of Muhammed Mustafa, the Messenger of Allah (may Allah bless him and his Ahlel-Bayt), from Makkah, had become the capital of Islam, had, at this time, a mixed population composed of three main groups, viz., the Muslim immigrants or refugees from Makkah; the original, Arab residents who had accepted Islam; and the Jews.

The Jews were also the original residents of Yathrib, now Medinah.

To each of the two groups of Muslims, Muhammed Mustafa, the Sovereign of Medina, gave a new name. To those Muslims who came with him from Makkah as refugees, he gave the name "Muhajireen," i.e., the "Immigrants," and to the Muslim tribes of Aus and Khazraj, he gave the name "Ansar," i.e. the "Supporters." The two groups were known by these names ever after, and they were very proud of them.

* * * * *

The Immigrants or the Refugees (Muhajireen) had lost their homes and all their material possessions in Makkah. In Medina, they were penniless. The Prophet of Islam had to find some way of integrating them into the social and economic life of Medina, and he had to do it soon.

In his efforts to rehabilitate the Immigrants (Muhajireen) in

67

the new city, one of the wrinkles adopted by the Prophet of Islam was to make them "brothers" of the Supporters (Ansar). He made one Immigrant the "brother" of one of the Supporters. Each of these supporters offered to share half of his land, property or wealth with his "brother" from Makkah. In their generosity, they outdid even the real, blood brothers of the Immigrants, and set an example which has no parallel in history.

Technically speaking, Salman the Persian was not an Immigrant from Makkah. But the Prophet found a "brother" for him also.

Following is the list of the pairs of "brothers:"

1. Muhammed Mustafa (S) and Ali ibn Abi Talib
2. Jaafer ibn Abi Talib and Maadh ibn Jabal
3. Abu Bakr Siddiq and Kharja ibn Zayd
4. Umar ibn al-Khattab and Utban ibn Malik
5. Uthman ibn Affan and Anas ibn Thabit
6. Abu Obeydah ibn al-Jarrah and Sa'ad ibn Ma'adh
7. Abdur Rahman ibn Auf and Sa'ad ibn ar-Rabi'i
8. Zubayr ibn al-Awwam and Salma ibn Salma
9. Talha ibn Ubaydullah and Ka'ab ibn Malik
10. Ammar ibn Yasser and Hudhayfa ibn al-Yaman
11. Abu Dharr el-Ghiffari and Mundhir ibn Amr
12. Salman el-Farsi and Abu-d-Darda
13. Saeed ibn Zayd and Ubbay ibn Ka'ab
14. Bilal and Ruwayha Abdullah ibn Abdur Rahman
15. Mas'ab ibn Umayr and Abu Ayub
16. Abu Hudhayfa ibn Utba ibn Rabia and Abbad ibn Bishr
17. Hatib ibn Abi Balta'a and Uwaym ibn Sa'ada

* * * * *

It is worthy of note that the first pair in this list, was made up, not by one Immigrant and one Supporter, but by Muhammed, the Messenger of Allah and Ali ibn Abi Talib - both Immigrants! It was the second time that Muhammed Mustafa, the Messenger of Allah, had declared that Ali was his brother. Earlier, he had made Ali his brother in Makkah.

* * * * *

A modern Indian historian, Qazi Suleyman Mansurpuri, says in his biography of the Prophet of Islam (may Allah bless him and his Ahlel-Bayt) that he had two reasons for making Ali his brother. "In the first place," he says, "Ali was his first cousin. In the second place, if he had called someone unrelated to him, his brother, it would have led to many difficult and complex problems in the times to come."

Jaafer ibn Abi Talib, the first cousin of Muhammed Mustafa and the elder brother of Ali, was not in Medina at this time; he was living in Abyssinia. Even so, the Prophet made him and Ma'adh ibn Jabal "brothers" of each other.

Perhaps it was compatibility in character and temperament of the parties that prompted Muhammed Mustafa to make them "brothers" of each other. Abu-d-Darda was made the "brother" of Salman because he shared the latter's devotion to the Messenger of Allah; the love of knowledge; contempt for a life of pleasure and luxury; and indifference to the seductions of economic and political power.

* * * * *

The long journey for Salman - both in space and in time - had come to an end. He had discovered the fountainhead of Eternal Truths and Everlasting Bliss in Islam, and he had become a personal friend of Muhammed Mustafa, the Messenger of Allah. The blessing of Islam had filled the chambers of his soul with the Light of Heaven. Islam was Allah's constant gift to him, and he delighted in its Beauty, Power and Sublimity. He felt that he had found the treasures of heaven and earth; he had found everything. Everything? Not quite! There was one thing that Salman had not found yet - his Freedom. He was still a slave. He could not measure the extent of his happiness when he was in the company of Muhammed Mustafa, the beloved of Allah. But when recollection came to him of his estate as a slave, he was roused as if he was stung by a wasp. His status as a slave hung like a dark and a sinister cloud over his life.

Muhammed Mustafa (may Allah bless him and his Ahlel-Bayt) who was a mercy for all Creation, was aware of Salman's distress, and suggested to him one day to ransom his freedom. Salman broached the subject to his master hoping that he would agree to set him free for a ransom. But the latter who knew that Salman had become a Muslim, refused to ransom him, and said: "If I set you free, you will most probably become a soldier in the army of Muhammed, and then you will fight against us. I shall, therefore, never emancipate you, and that will mean one enemy-in-arms less for us."

Salman was heart-broken to hear his master's response. He, however, reported it to Muhammed Mustafa who advised him to be patient, and to put his trust in Allah's mercy, Who (he said) would remove his distress.

BUT THOSE WHO BELIEVE AND WORK DEEDS OF RIGHTEOUSNESS, AND BELIEVE IN THE (REVELATION) SENT DOWN TO MUHAMMED - FOR IT IS THE TRUTH FROM THEIR LORD, - HE WILL REMOVE FROM THEM ILLS AND WILL IMPROVE THEIR CONDITION.

(Quran Majid. Chapter 47; verse 2)

The cloud of despondency lifted for Salman, and he returned to his oasis with a merry heart, knowing that what the blessed

Messenger of Allah had said, could never be wrong, and therefore, the day when he would become free, could not be too distant.

* * * * *

One reason why Salman agonised over his estate as a slave, was that it robbed him of the opportunity to serve Allah and His Messenger, Muhammed Mustafa. He was especially desolate in those critical moments when Islam was challenged by its external foes, and he could not be present at the scene of action to face them. It was after his conversion to Islam that the polytheists of Makkah posed a threat to the physical existence of the little community of the Muslims in Medina, in the battlefields of Badr and Uhud. Salman wished more than anyone else to take part in those battles and to defend Muhammed Mustafa from his enemics; but his master, Uthman bin Ashhel, did not allow him to leave the oasis. He lamented the loss of merits because of his inability to be present in those battles.

* * * * *

In A.D. 622 when Muhammed Mustafa (may Allah bless him and his Ahlel-Bayt) came to Yathrib (=Medina), as an Immigrant, there were the two Arab tribes of Aus and Khazraj, and three Jewish tribes of Qaynuqa'a, Nadhir and Qurayza, living in that city, as noted before.

The two Arab tribes accepted Islam, and they became the proud hosts and supporters (=Ansar) of the Messenger of Allah and the Immigrants (Muhajireen). Both of them - the hosts in Medina, and the guests from Makkah - formed the nucleus of the nascent Muslim community. It was around this community that the Islamic State and the Government were destined to take shape in the years to come.

To the Jews, however, the ideology of Islam, was not acceptable.

But no pressure, direct or indirect, was applied on them to accept it. Muhammed Mustafa granted them the famous "Charter of Medina." This Charter guaranteed their civil and religious rights, and recognized their right to live - with other Muslims - as members of autonomous tribes.

In return, the Jews acknowledged Muhammed Mustafa as the political sovereign of Medina, and they agreed to defend the city with the Muslims in the event of an invasion by an external enemy. They also agreed, not to give any aid, moral and/or material, to the enemies of Islam, especially to the Quraysh - the idolaters of Makkah.

But as subsequent events were to show very soon, the Jews did not have much respect for the Charter of Medina. Many among them became active spies for the Quraysh. Their poets instigated the latter to attack Medina, and hinted that they (the Jews) would aid them. It soon became clear to the Muslims that in an exigency, the Jews would sabotage the defences of Islam, and would engineer its destruction from within. They (the Jews) were, therefore, much more dangerous to the security of the City-State of Medina than the pagans of Arabia who were the overt enemies of Islam.

It was for these reasons that the tribe of Qaynuqa'a was expelled from Medina after the battle of Badr. The tribe of Nadhir was banished after the battle of Uhud. The conduct of both tribes had been highly treasonable.

After the banishment of Qaynuqa'a and Nadhir, Qurayza was the only Jewish tribe left in Medina. Uthman bin Ashhel also belonged to the Qurayza. The action against Qaynuqa'a and Nadhir had made him a little less unreasonable than he had been in the past. Therefore, when Salman broached the subject of paying ransom for his freedom once again, he (Uthman) was willing to listen, and he was willing to negotiate the terms of his emancipation with him.

72

Uthman specified to Salman the price of his freedom. Salman would have to plant in Uthman's gardens, three hundred young date-palms, and he would pay him 40 oz. of gold.

Salman presented these terms to Muhammed Mustafa. The latter, thereupon, turned to his companions, and said to them: "Assist your brother."

All the companions rose to assist their brother. One of them brought thirty saplings; another brought twenty; a third brought fifteen; a fourth ten, and so on, until they had collected all three hundred as required by the Jew.

The Prophet then ordered the companions to dig the earth in which the saplings were to be planted. When the ground was ready for planting, he himself came, and planted the first tree with his own hands. Then the companions took charge of the project, and planted the other trees. Every tree struck roots, and not one out of the three hundred was lost.

Three hundred date-palms were planted in the garden of Uthman bin Ashhel but Salman still had to pay 40 oz. of gold to him. He was not free yet.

A few more weeks passed, and then one day Muhammed Mustafa (may Allah bless him and his Ahlel-Bayt) sent for Salman. When the latter came into the Mosque, he noticed that he was seated on the floor, and his companions sat around him. In front of him there was a tray and in the tray there were some nuggets of gold.

The Messenger of Allah said to Salman: "Take this gold and give it to your master. This is the balance of your ransom."

Salman, who was obviously surprised to see so much gold, exclaimed:

"O Messenger of Allah! How shall I ever repay so much gold?"

The Messenger of Allah only repeated the command, and told Salman to "leave the rest to Allah."

The gold, it turned out, was exactly 40 oz. in weight. Salman gave it to Uthman bin Ashhel, and was emancipated. At length, Salman the Persian was a free man once again, thanks to Allah and His Messenger. It were both of them - Allah and His Messenger - who had set in motion the process which culminated in the emancipation of Salman after long and painful years of slavery. How could he ever thank both of them?

BUT GOD WILL DELIVER THE RIGHTEOUS
TO THEIR PLACE OF SALVATION:
NO EVIL SHALL TOUCH THEM, NOR SHALL
THEY GRIEVE.

(Quran Majid. Chapter 39; verse 61)

Suddenly everything changed for Salman. The gulf between slavery and freedom had appeared to him to be unfathomable and unbridgeable. But he had called Allah and His Messenger for aid. They had responded, and with their aid, he had cleared the "gulf." The stifling and noisome air of slavery had suddenly changed into the fresh and revitalizing air of freedom for him.

Suddenly, the years fell, like scales, from Salman's shoulders. Suddenly, the spring, the bounce, the vigor and the sheen of youth returned to him. Incredible was the resiliency of his buoyant spirit.

The recent past of Salman's life, dominated as it was, by the sinister figure of a slave-owner, had been a nightmare for him; but his present felicity in his triumph in recovering his freedom, had crowded the trauma of slavery out of his consciousnees.

The dark and menacing clouds of the past, had dissolved in the glorious light of Islam, and in the life-giving ambience of Freedom.

Islam and Freedom had extricated Salman from the vast wilderness of time which his past had been until then, and from that moment, he became "future-oriented," as five years earlier, he had become "Islam-oriented."

After his emancipation from the slavery of a Jew, Salman the Persian became a slave once again - voluntarily. This time he chose his own masters, and they were Allah and His Messenger, Muhammed Mustafa. This new "slavery" became his greatest pride and his greatest pleasure. He wore it as a badge of distinction, and he was not willing to exchange it even for the empire of the "Seven Climates."

As noted before, Salman found his slavery to Allah and to His Messenger, Muhammed Mustafa (may Allah bless him and his Ahlel-Bayt) extremely delectable and he wanted to spend every moment of his life waiting upon them. Once he entered their service, he adopted the following "credo" as his new philosophy of life:

> *(Say): "VERILY, MY LORD HATH GUIDED ME TO A WAY THAT IS STRAIGHT, - A RELIGION OF RIGHT, - THE PATH (TROD) BY ABRAHAM, THE TRUE IN FAITH, AND HE WAS NOT ONE OF THOSE WHO ASSOCIATE PARTNERS WITH GOD."*

> *(Say): "TRULY, MY PRAYER AND MY SERVICE OF SACRIFICE, MY LIFE AND MY DEATH, ARE (ALL) FOR ALLAH, THE CHERISHER OF THE WORLDS; NO PARTNER HATH HE; THIS I AM COMMANDED, AND I AM THE FIRST OF THOSE WHO BOW TO HIS WILL."*

> (Quran Majid. Chapter 6; verses 161-163)

* * * * *

Salman had an insatiable thirst for knowledge. As a slave, in personal attendance on Muhammed Mustafa, the Messenger of Allah (may Allah bless him and his Ahlel-Bayt), he had access, at all times, to the Fountainhead of all Knowledge. He could "drink deep" at it, and he did, to his heart's content and delight. But he was not entirely satisfied with what he had been able to accomplish for himself. He knew that there were those men and women who were eager to grasp the Truth but who had no access to the Fountainhead of Knowledge as he had. He, therefore, wanted to share with them the bounties that Allah had given him by elevating him to the high rank of a companion of His Messenger, Muhammed Mustafa. He was very anxious that those Muslims who did not have knowledge of the Arabic language, such as his own Persian compatriots, should also become recipients of the blessings of Quran Majid through comprehension of its message, and assimilation of its content.

He, therefore, decided to translate Quran Majid into Persian. Sarakhsi tells us in his *Mabsut* (Volume I, page 37), that with the approval and encouragement of his master, Muhammed Mustafa (may Allah bless him and his Ahlel-Bayt), Salman translated into Persian, selected passages of Quran Majid for the immediate requirements and benefit of the Persian (=Iranian) converts to Islam. This makes him the pioneer of all translators of the Book of Allah. He brought the blessings of that Book - cosmic in its source, universal in its reach - to the people of Iran in their own idiom.

* * * * *

Muhammed Mustafa, the Messenger of Allah (may Allah bless him and his Ahlel-Bayt), called Salman "the First Gift of Iran to Islam."

Salman was indeed a most splendid "gift" of Iran to Islam, as he was very soon to prove - during the siege of Medina by the pagan army of Makkah in A.D. 627 - and an indispensable one!

May Allah bless Salman and may He be pleased with him.

* * * * *

Chapter VI

The Battle of Ahzab or the Siege of Medina - Feb-March 627

The battle of Uhud had been fought in early 625. In that battle, the polytheists of Makkah had defeated the Muslims. But the victors had been unable to follow up their victory. They realized, a little too late, that the fruits of their victory had all been lost.

Once this realization dawned upon the pagan leaders in Makkah, the decided to do something about it instead of lamenting the loss of the fruits of victory. They agreed, by consensus, that the only way to make restitutions for their past errors and failures was to wage a new war upon the Muslims, and to carry it, this time, into Medina itself.

The pagans spent two years in mobilizing men and materials on a vast scale. At the end of two years, they felt confident that they were strong enough to challenge any foe - in Arabia or elsewhere.

* * * * *

Salman the Persian had just redeemed his freedom when Medina, the capital of Islam, was threatened by an unprecedented peril. In early February 627, Muhammed Mustafa, the Prophet of Islam (may Allah bless him and his Ahlel-Bayt), received intelligence that the polytheists of Makkah had completed their preparations for an invasion of Medina with a cavalry and an infantry of ten thousand seasoned warriors of Arabia, and he also learned that their resolution was to obliterate Islam in one massive, coordinated attack.

When the Muslims heard these reports, they were seized with panic. Medina had no means to defend itself from such a formidable army, the largest ever assembled in Arabia until then. The Prophet called an emergency meeting of his principal companions to consult them in what manner to defend Medina.

Medina had natural or man-made defences on three sides but was exposed on one side - the north. If the enemy decided to enter the city from the north, there was nothing to stop him.

Lieutenant-General Sir John Glubb, the British historian of the Arabs, says that the Arabs had no experience in siege warfare. The only mode of fighting with which they had familiarity, was the one called "hit-and-run" of the desert warfare. The Arabic phrase *karr-o-farr* means "attack-and-run," and that's how the Arabs fought. They attacked an enemy and then they ran, before the latter had time to recover from surprise.

It was the hope of the Makkan generals that they would capture Medina in a surprise and lightning raid.

The Makkan generals might have captured Medina with their strategy but for the presence in that city of a "foreigner" - Salman the Persian. He worked out a strategy of his own, and his counter-strategy foiled the Makkan strategy. He had observed the siege operations of the Persians and the Romans in their interminable wars against each other, and he had the ability to make scientific deductions from his observations. He pitted his knowledge of "static" warfare against the invaders and succeeded in checkmating them. He said to the prophet that if a trench, too deep and too wide for the horses to leap over, were dug on the exposed section of the perimeter of the city, it would immobilize the enemy cavalry.

The trench was a novel idea, unfamiliar to the Arabs. But the

Prophet immediately grasped its significance, and ordered Muslims to start digging. Work was begun under the direction of Salman. Since the enemy host was known to have left Makkah already, there was not a moment to lose. Digging went on non-stop, in relays and shifts, night and day.

Muhammad Husayn Haykal writes in his book *The Life of Muhammad*, published in Cairo (Egypt) in 1935:

> "Salman el-Farsi had more knowledge of the techniques of warfare than anyone else in the Peninsula. He advised the digging of a trench around Medina and the fortification of the buildings within. The Muslims hurried to implement this advice. The trench was dug and the Prophet worked with his own hands alongside his companions lifting the earth, encouraging the workers, and urging everyone to redouble his effort."

Salman himself was very eager to outdo all others at digging. He astonished everyone by his prodigious strength. He was indefatigable. Muhammad ibn Umar al-Waqidi, the Arab historian, says that he alone worked as much as six other men.

Salman was not one of those Muslims who came with the Prophet from Makkah, and whom he (the Prophet) gave the name *Muhajireen* (Immigrants), as noted before. Salman came to Yathrib as a slave long before the Muslims came from Makkah.

When the trench was being dug, one of the Muhajireen who was watching Salman, claimed him as a Muhajir (Immigrant from Makkah). "Salman is one of us, Muhajireen," he said. But he was at once challenged by the Muslims of Medina (the Ansar) when they heard this claim, and one of them said: "No. Salman is one of us, Ansar."

A lively argument began between the two groups of Muslims - the Muhajireen and the Ansar - each of them claiming that Salman belonged to their group, and not to the other group.

Presently, the Apostle of Allah arrived on the scene, and he too heard the argument of the Muhajireen and the Ansar. He was amused by the claims of the two sides but he soon put an end to their argument by saying:

> "Salman is neither a Muhajir nor an Ansar. He is one of *us*. He is one of the People of the House."

Muhammed ibn Ishaq, the earliest biographer of the Prophet of Islam, writes in his famous Seera (Life of the Messenger of God):

> "It is said that Salman the Persian advised the Apostle to make the trench. A traditionist told me that on this day the Muhajireen claimed that Salman belonged to them, while the Ansar said that he was their man, but the Apostle said: Salman belongs to us, the People of the House.'"

The Arab historian, Kamil ibn Atheer, has also quoted the Messenger of Allah in his book, *Tarikh Kamil* (History, Vol. 2, page 122), as saying:

"Salman is one of us. He is a member of our household."

This is the greatest honor ever bestowed upon anyone by Muhammed Mustafa, the Messenger of Allah. As recipient of revelation from Heaven, and as its interpreter, he declared that Salman was a member of his house - the Family of the Chosen ones of Allah. No one else in the entire history of Islam has ever been elevated to such a high rank as Salman the Persian.

Hardly the last spadeful of earth had been cast out of the trench, when the cavaliers of Makkah arrived, thundering across the desert - like a whirlwind. But suddenly they were checked in their career by a strange new obstacle - the trench. What was it? They had never seen anything like it before. The riders reined in their horses at its edge to examine it. They had expected their momentum to carry them into the heart of Medina but there was this chasm yawning between them and their objective, and too deep and too wide, they noted, for their horses to negotiate.

The pagan generals were disconcerted and dismayed by this unconventional tactic adopted by the Muslims to defend their city. The tactic - the trench - immobilized them, just as Salman had predicted, and they were at a loss to know what to do or how to circumvent it. One of them said: "This is the work of that Persian; the Arabs did not know it." Finally, they decided to lay siege to Medina, and to starve it into surrender. With this aim, they sealed all its exits, and made it impossible for anyone to carry food or any other supplies into it.

The siege of Medina might have lasted a long time with unpredictable results but it did not. One of the Makkan generals - Amr ibn Abd Wudd - lost patience with this "static" or "un-Arab" mode of fighting, and he decided to change its character by hurdling the trench, and by carrying a "dynamic" or an "Arab" war into the camp of the Muslims.

Amr ibn Abd Wudd and three of his staff officers, therefore, went on an inspection of the trench from one end to the other. At one point they discovered a rocky projection in it which the Muslims had been unable to cut. It looked to them as if their horses could leap over the trench from that rock. They made some rough calculations to judge the width of the trench, and satisfied themselves that they could clear it; retreated from its edge, and spurred their horses. The horses galloped; their hoofs came to rest upon the rock for a moment, and then leapt over the trench. All four of them cleared it, thus landing inside the city!

Amr ibn Abd Wudd was the most famous hero of pagan Arabia. M. Shibli, the Indian historian, and Abbas Mahmood al-Akkad, the Egyptian historian, write in their histories that Amr was reckoned as more than a match for a thousand warriors. Once inside the perimeter of the city, he boldly advanced toward the encampment of the Muslims, and challenged them to single combat in the classical tradition of Arabian warfare.

The prestige of Amr's name as a warrior was so high in Arabia that it was enough to strike terror into the hearts of his enemies. And now when he recklessly leapt over the trench and challenged the champions of the Muslims from their own doorstep, they were paralysed with fear. No one among them dared to take up his insolent challenge, knowing it to be the sentence of inevitable death.

Amr challenged the Muslims a second time but was again greeted only by silence.

Amr prowled restlessly in front of the Muslim camp. A few minutes later, he challenged the Muslims for the third time. He taunted them for their cowardice but also promised to send them to paradise if they came out and fought against him.

Still there was no answer.

It must have seemed to Amr ibn Abd Wudd and to the Makkan knights with him that no one in the camp of the Muslims was very eager to enter paradise by accepting his challenge.

Quran Majid has drawn a portrait of the state of the Muslims at this time in the following verses:

> BEHOLD! THEY CAME ON YOU FROM ABOVE YOU
> AND FROM BELOW YOU, AND BEHOLD, THE EYES
> BECAME DIM AND THE HEARTS GAPED UP TO
> THE
> THROATS, AND YE IMAGINED VARIOUS (VAIN)
> THOUGHTS ABOUT ALLAH!
> IN THAT SITUATION WERE THE BELIEVERS TRIED;
> THEY WERE SHAKEN AS BY A TREMENDOUS
> SHAKING.

(Chapter 33; verses 10,11)

Truly, Amr had put the Muslims in a state of suspended

animation. Most of them hoped that their silence would save their necks from his sword.

What Amr did not know at this time was that in the camp of the Muslims, there was a young man who had volunteered to accept his (Amr's) very first challenge but Muhammed Mustafa had restrained him, and had ordered him to wait. The young man in question was Ali ibn Abi Talib, the cousin of the Prophet. He was in his mid-twenties at the time.

When Amr challenged the Muslims a second time, Ali rose again, and volunteered to go out and to meet him. But once again the Prophet beckoned him to wait.

Then came Amr's third challenge, and still no one in the camp of the Muslims responded to it except Ali.

Amr was gloating over the discomfiture of the Muslims. He rode his prancing horse in front of the Muslim camp, coming at times, uncomfortably close. Getting no answer to his challenge, he hurled his javelin at the tent of the Prophet of Islam himself.

The Prophet resented Amr's insolence and his cockiness. He had given ample opportunity to the heroes of the Muslims to prove their mettle but they had decided to act upon the dictates of prudence. Their silence was a dictate of their prudence.

The prudence of the Muslims left no choice for Muhammed Mustafa but to let Ali ibn Abi Talib take up the challenge of Amr ibn Abd Wudd. He could not afford to let the pagan challenge to Islam go unanswered.

Ali put on the armor and the helmet of Muhammed Mustafa, the Messenger of Allah. The latter himself suspended the famous sword - *Dhul-Fiqar* - (the Piercer), to his side, said a prayer for his victory, and committed him to the protection of Allah.

If Amr ibn Abd Wudd was the greatest hero of paganism, Ali was the greatest hero of Islam. But Ali was also the greatest missionary of Islam. Whenever he encountered an adversary, he offered him the following three options before fighting:

1. Accept Islam. Declare that Allah is One and Muhammed is His Messenger. Doing so would be in your interest in this world and in the Hereafter.
2. If you do not wish to accept Islam, then withdraw from the battlefield. Do not wage war upon the Messenger of Allah. Fighting against him will bring damnation upon you in the two worlds.
3. If the second option also is not acceptable to you, then the third and the last option for you is to strike at me, since I cannot be the first one to strike at you.

Amr rejected the first two options with disdain. As for the third, he said, he would accept it. But the "option" made him roar with laughter, and he said that he had not believed that anyone on the face of the earth would dare to invite him to be the first to strike at him (at the foe).

Amr, the most consummate swordsman of the infidels, then lifted his ponderous sword, and brought it down on Ali's head with irresistible force. His sword cut through the shield, the helmet and the turban of Ali, and made a deep gash in his forehead.

A stream of blood leapt out of Ali's forehead but he was not dismayed. He quickly rallied, and struck a counter-blow with *Dhul-Fiqar* which killed Amr ibn Abd Wudd, the kingpin of the heroes of pagan Arabia.

Ali held his sword high and shouted "Allah-o-Akbar." That lusty yell of triumph sent a frisson of excitement through the host of Islam. At the same time it cast a pall over the invading army.

As soon as Amr fell to the ground, the other three knights who had accompanied him, hastily retreated across the trench. Ali let them retreat. It was against his principles to pursue a fleeing enemy.

The death of Amr ibn Abd Wudd was the death blow to the morale and the will-to-fight of the Makkan army. All its hopes for a quick victory over the Muslims had lain in him, and with his death, it began to fall apart.

The pagan army had not recovered from the shock of Amr's death yet when the weather turned sour. First it became unseasonably cold, and then a violent sand storm arose which blew in the faces of the Makkans. It was plain to see that they could not withstand its fury for long. They lost their elan and they began to desert or to disperse, first in twos and threes, then in tens and twenties, and finally, in hundreds. The alliance of the Makkans and the other pagan tribes broke up; the army of the invaders began to dissolve visibly, and the threat to the security of Medina was averted

Medina was saved from annihilation. But one shudders to contemplate what might have happened if the trench had not been dug. The ten thousand wild tribesmen would have taken the city by storm, and they would have slaughtered every Muslim in it. The defenders would have been overwhelmed by sheer numbers. By killing all Muslims - men, women and children - the pagans would have snuffed Islam out of existence, and thus would have achieved their aim.

The invasion of Medina in 627 by the pagans of Makkah, has been called by Quran Majid as (the Battle of) Ahzab (the Confederates). Most historiàns call it the Battle of Khandaq (the Trench). And it is also known as the Siege of Medina.

Amin Dawidar, the modern Egyptian historian, writes in his biography of the Prophet of Islam, published in Cairo (Egypt) in 1953 as follows:

> "The battle of Ahzab was not a 'conventional' battle in which the heroes of the two sides attacked each other, and then withdrew. It was not a battle in which troops advanced and retreated. It was a battle of nerves. It was a test of the endurance and stamina of the Muslims; it was a test of their resolution and faith; it was a test of their moral as well as their physical

courage; it was a test of their morale.

"They passed the test.

"But there is absolutely no doubt that it was the mercy of Allah alone which saved the Muslims in the Battle of Ahzab. Had His mercy not protected them, they would have been massacred, and the Great Design of Islam would have become a fiasco."

But the Muslims and Islam were saved from such a fate. Allah works through His slaves. He made His slave, Salman the Persian, the "instrument" through which He saved the Muslim Umma (community). Salman's wits proved to be the best defence of Islam in the Siege of Medina. His role that led to the debacle of the army of the infidels besieging Medina, makes him unique among all the companions of Muhammed Mustafa, the Messenger of Allah (may Allah bless him and his family).

Allah had planned a mission, and His slave, Salman the Persian, carried it out for Him.

* * * * *

The failure of the Siege of Medina in 627 was a most significant event in the history of Islam and of Arabia. It meant that the infidels of Makkah would never be able to mount another invasion of Medina - the fortress of Islam. The successful defence of Medina, made Islam "invulnerable." After the battle of Ahzab, the initiative passed, finally and irreversibly, from the infidels of Makkah to the Muslims of Medina, and Islam was able to move into a position of dominance in the Peninsula.

* * * * *

Muhammed Mustafa, the Messenger of Allah (may Allah bless him and his Ahlel-Bayt) had many companions; but Salman

86

was a "special" among them all, as noted before. The other companions also knew about the rapport that existed between him and his master, and in all unforeseen or unforeseeable situations, counted upon his resourcefulness for assistance. One day an old woman of Medina stopped Muhammed Mustafa on the street, and started pouring out a long and pointless story before him. He heard patiently. But the story became endless. Presently the time came for prayer but he was still unable to disengage himself. The companions were waiting; they became worried, and they requested Salman to go to find him, and to bring him to the Mosque.

Salman arrived at the scene. In his customary and disarming manner, he told the old lady that he too wanted to hear her story, and that she ought to tell the rest of it to him. His timely intervention enabled the Messenger of Allah to return to the Mosque.

From time to time, some hungry wayfarer wandered into Medina. Not knowing where to go, he invariably repaired to the Mosque, and asked the Prophet to feed him. At this point, Salman took charge. He gently shepherded the hungry guest out of the Mosque and fed him. His love for the Prophet was forever struggling to find expression, and impelled him to "protect" him in all such minor but time-consuming situations. It was well-known in Medina that Salman was a multi-talented man. To his many talents, he added the rare quality of address so that he invariably did the right thing in the right way at the right time.

* * * * *

Slavery had been a negative and an inhibiting factor in the life of Salman, as in the life of all other slaves. It is possible that he had deferred his marriage until the time when he would be free again. In course of time, Allah and His Messenger were pleased to bestow the great and the incomparable gift of freedom upon him, and he decided to marry. Sibt ibn al-Jauzi, an Arab historian, says that Salman married a woman of the tribe of Beni Kinda, and he had a son from her. The son's name was Abdullah. It is from this circumstance that he was called Abu Abdullah (=the father of Abdullah), as per the custom of the Arabs.

* * * * *

It was and still is a custom of the Arabs to identify a man or a woman by the name of his or her father - ibn or bint (=son or daughter) of so-and-so. In Medina, a stranger once stopped Salman on the street, and asked him the name of his father. "Islam," answered Salman. "The name of my father," he further elucidated, "is Islam. I am Salman ibn Islam (=Salman the son of Islam)."

When Salman said that he was the "son of Islam," he was not using a figure of speech for its dramatic effect. He was not even trying to accent his profound attachment to Islam. He was only stating a plain truth. It was not only he who had fallen under the "spell" of Islam, and had adopted its genius; it was also the genius of Islam that had "adopted" him. The incident, however, points up Salman's mystique of love for Islam more eloquently than massive volumes. There was an inner harmony - an affinity - between the personal destiny of Salman and Islam. Islam was the synthesis of his emotions, and he was a part of its "blood-stream." His pure and sainted life was perfectly integrated with Islam. In thought, word, deed, character and personality, he had achieved total identification with Islam. In a very real sense, he was a "product" of Islam!

Salman left everything for Islam. He forgot every connection, such as the connection of family or nation, for the connection of Islam. He endured every privation for Islam. He relinquished every honor so he could receive the honors that Islam alone could bestow upon him.

Through obedience to Allah, and devotion to His Messenger, Muhammed Mustafa (may Allah bless him and his Ahlel-Bayt), Salman lifted himself into immortality. He lives in the hearts of the Faithful.

Chapter VII

The Death of Muhammed Mustafa, the Messenger of Allah

Muhammed Mustafa (may Allah bless him and his Ahlel-Bayt) was the unquestioned benefactor of all mankind; he was also the leader and benefactor of all Muslims; and he was the leader, benefactor and friend of Salman the Persian. On June 8, 632, he died in Medina at the age of 63 years. Salman was crushed by sorrow, and his heart was splintered.

Muhammed Mustafa was the sun and the moon of the world of Salman, and with his death, it was plunged into darkness. Salman had known disaster and tragedy in life but the loss of his friend, Muhammed Mustafa, was the most staggering blow to him ever. It was a shock from which, he thought, he might never recover. He felt as if he might lose his grip on life itself.

Salman was totally disoriented. We do not know how long did this titanic sorrow last for him but at length, reality began to consolidate itself once again. He realized that he still had many duties to carry out which Allah and His Messenger,

Muhammed Mustafa himself had imposed upon him. Therefore, slowly, painfully and laboriously, he began to rally, and by degrees, he returned to the world of the living. But that world, without Muhammed in it, was desolate in his sight.

It was through Muhammed Mustafa, the Beloved of Allah, that Salman had received the greatest of all blessings in the world - the blessing of Islam. Muhammed Mustafa had rescued him from the sin of false worship. By doing so, he (Muhammed) had guaranteed his (Salman's) welfare, success and happiness in this world, and in the Hereafter.

But this was not all!

Salman had also received, through Muhammed Mustafa (may Allah bless him and his Ahlel-Bayt), the second greatest blessing of Allah on this earth - the blessing of Freedom. Muhammed had rescued him from the clutches of a rapacious slave-owner. Nothing could match for Salman the thrill of Freedom. Freedom was a sensation that he savored every moment eversince his benefactor, Muhammed Mustafa, had paid the ransom for him, and his master - Uthman bin Ashhel - had emancipated him.

But this was not all!

Muhammed Mustafa, the Messenger of Allah, was the greatest sovereign in world history. He was also the most condescending sovereign. He held Salman by the hand, led him into his court, and bestowed upon him the lofty rank of his courtier. As a courtier of Muhammed Mustafa, the Beloved of Allah, Salman waited on him every moment, and every one of those moments was a manifestation of rapture for him. During the years when Salman was a courtier of Muhammed Mustafa, he reached the zenith of his devotional life, and he stayed there.

Muhammed Mustafa was a sovereign who "pampered" Salman.

Then the sovereign died. His death, as noted before, was a catastrophe for Salman. Suddenly the "court" ceased to exist, and suddenly the "courtiers" were all dispersed.

Salman's sense of loss, at the death of the master who "pampered" him, was incalculably stupendous.

Salman owed Muhammed Mustafa everything in his life.

He was 65-years old when his master died.

Chapter VIII

Salman as Governor of Madaen

Next to Muhammed Mustafa, the Messenger of Allah (may Allah bless him and his Ahlel-Bayt), his first cousin, Ali ibn Abi Talib, was the focus of Salman's love and devotion. The love of Muhammed and Ali was. for him, the perpetual and unfailing touchstone of the faith of a Muslim. Ali, to him, was the interpreter, par excellence, of Quran Majid, and of the life and the ideals of his friend and master, Muhammed Mustafa, the Messenger of Allah. He loved and served Ali with the same zeal as he had served Muhammed Mustafa. He knew that Allah and Muhammed loved Ali, and he shared, with both of them, their love for him (Ali).

* * * * *

After the death of Muhammed Mustafa, Salman went into "retirement" from the world. For almost a quarter of a century, he lived "incognito." Very little, if anything, is known about what he did or how he lived during those years. He appears to have been anxious only not to attract any attention. He spent his time in prayer, and he made his living by making and selling handicrafts of palm-leaf, and he shared his earnings with the poor and the destitute.

* * * * *

In June 656, Ali ibn Abi Talib ascended the throne of caliphate in Medina as the successor of Muhammed Mustafa, the Messenger of Allah (may Allah bless him and his Ahlel-Bayt). One of his first acts, upon taking charge of the government of the Muslims, was to appoint Salman el-Farsi the governor of the city and the district of Madaen in Iraq.

All his life, Salman had cherished the vision of his master, Muhammed, of a world of justice and a world of peace. He, therefore, welcomed his appointment as governor as an opportunity to share that vision with the umma of his master.

At this time, Salman was quite advanced in years. But thanks to his abstemiousness, and to the Spartan discipline he had imposed upon himself all his life, he was in top physical condition. In fact, physically, it appeared that he was untouched by time or by the rigors of his own life. His mental faculties were also sharp and clear as ever. He remained spry and lucid to the end of his life. Perhaps, in prayer he had found the secret of halting decadence. Prayer for him was a process of restoration and renewal that he applied constantly to his life, especially in moments of personal upheaval. For him it was an antidote to the wear and tear of existence.

The governor-designate left Medina on his 800-miles long journey across the great Arabian desert, accompanied by only a guide. His baggage consisted of a "sajjada" made of palm-leaf on which to say prayers, a bag containing crusts of barley bread, a water-bag made of goat-skin, a cup and a pillow. These were all his worldly possessions. He was carrying all of them to Madaen with him, and he had left nothing behind him in Medina.

* * * * *

At night, Salman halted at an inn in an oasis for saying his prayers and for resting. He was thirsty and he was going to drink water from his cup when he saw a man drinking water from a scoop of his hands. Salman looked at his cup and said: This cup is useless for me. I can also drink water from my hands." Saying this, he decided to discard the cup.

Later, Salman saw another traveller who was sleeping with his head resting upon his forearm. Salman, who was getting ready to sleep, looked at his pillow, and said: "This pillow is useless for me. I can also sleep with my head resting on my arm." Saying this, he decided to dispense with his pillow.

The cup and the pillow suddenly seemed to Salman to be encumbrances, and he made them a gift to a poor wayfarer. He did not want to burden himself with too many non-essentials. He had an abhorrence of clutter - of possessions that weigh down a man's otherwise free spirit. He did not want to be a "prisoner" of material goods, and looked beyond the parameters of finite resources to a system in which matter ceases to be a factor.

When Salman reached the environs of Madaen, he saw a vast multitude of people who had turned out in their most flamboyant finery. The news of his appointment and arrival, had apparently preceded him into Madaen, and its citizens had come out to greet him - their new governor. They expected to see him escorted into Madaen by glittering cavalry, infantry and body-guards; with banners and pennants snapping in the air over his head; and in full panoply of power and authority.

When the citizens of Madaen saw two camel-riders approaching toward them from the direction of Medina, they thought that they might know where the new governor was. When the camel-riders came near them, they eagerly asked one of them if he had seen the new governor or if he had heard anything about him. He pointed to the other camel-rider, and said: "He is your new governor."

The citizens were surprised to hear this and they did not believe him. They thought he was being facetious and saucy. How could a solitary camel-rider be their governor, and where was all the pomp and pageantry which had accompanied his predecessors, if he was the governor, they asked.

It was not until Salman had produced the letter of appointment which Ali ibn Abi Talib had given him, that the citizens of Madaen were convinced that he was their new governor.

The dignitaries of Madaen escorted Salman to the Government House - the official residence of their governors. Salman was much "impressed" by the edifice but shied away from it. To the dignitaries he said that the Government House was much too grandiose for him, and that he would be much more comfortable in a more modest dwelling. He instinctively rebelled against expansive living.

The dignitaries offered to Salman some other houses which were less pretentious than the Government House but he thought that the walls of masonry would inhibit the poor. He did not want the walls of his house to become barriers between himself and them.

Salman then selected a tiny lot which was vacant near the center of Madaen, swept it clean of shrubs and other detritus, brought reeds from the flaggy marshes nearby, and set to work to construct for himself a frail "frame-house" of thatch. It was going to be his home, his court and his guest-house for as long as he was going to be the governor of Madaen.

The pickets, the sentinels and the watchdogs guarding the gates of the palaces and the fortresses of their masters, have terrified the poor and the weak for thousands of years. Salman unconsciously feared lest the poor and the weak equate him also with those tyrants whose minions terrified them. In building a cottage of thatch, therefore, he was prompted by his desire to be accessible at all times to each and all - high and low, rich and poor, strong and weak - in his wilayat (Madaen and the areas around it under his jurisdiction).

By his unconventional attitude toward the relations between

the rulers and the ruled, Salman shocked the rich and the mighty; he surprised the poor and the weak; and, without a doubt, he won the pleasure of the Creator.

Salman wanted to change the character of the relationship between the rulers and the ruled. When power came into his hands, a strange thing happened, viz., it were not his "subjects" who showed any eagerness to ingratiate themselves with him; it was he who showed eagerness to "ingratiate" himself with them, especially, with those who were the chronically "under-privileged" among them.

Salman had been a Roman citizens for more than thirty years. In those years, he had studied, at first hand, the political and the social organization of the Roman State. He knew that hierarchies of status and authority - the "pecking orders" of social dominance and prestige - existed in Rome as they did in Persia. These "pecking orders" are, in fact, inherent in all social systems, and they are established by "pecking." But Salman considered them an iniquity, and he was resolved to change them.

Conventional belief sees man as created by God but thrust into a world in which political and economic forces largely determine the quality of his life. Salman wished to change this old perception. He didn't want man to be at the mercy of political and economic forces. He believed that the quality of the life of a Muslim ought to be determined only by the command-ments and prohibitions of Quran Majid. To change the old perception, therefore, the first thing he did when he became governor, was to divest the governmental authority of its air of "awe" and its spurious pomposity. He was going to make the government which controls political and economic forces, a slave of the Muslims, as far as it was within his power to do so.

But Salman did not make a deliberate attempt to breed, in the minds of the masses, any contempt for the government. He only wished that the weak, the humble, and the oppressed would have absolutely no fear of the governmental apparatus, and that they would have absolutely no hesitation in coming to see him, addressing him as an equal, and demanding redress of their grievances. He also wished to put an end to "private imperialism" by extirpating the "sharks" who live by preying upon simple and gullible people. He turned his hands, his head and his heart to anything that promised to yield safety, comfort, hope, cheer and security to them.

Security is the proper business of the government. But by security, Salman didn't mean security merely from aggression by external invaders, or from crime by miscreants and lawless men at home, but also from such enemies of mankind as poverty, hunger, disease and ignorance.

One of the aims of Salman as governor of Madaen was to insinuate the egalitarian mechanism of Islam into every detail of the life of the Muslims. Any distinction among them, on grounds of economic and/or social privilege, smacked to him of treason to Islam.

Salman also considered it his duty, as governor, to be as close to the poor, the weak and the humble, in terms of shared values and heritage, as possible. He was, in fact, most anxious to convince them that they were far more important than he - Salman, the governor of Madaen - was! He firmly believed that his pleasure was not important for them but that their pleasure was absolutely indispensable for his own salvation on the day of the final reckoning when he would be standing in the Tribunal of the Creator.

This was baseline knowledge for Salman, the governor of Madaen.

* * * * *

When Salman first came to Yathrib as a slave, many years

earlier, he had taught himself the craft of "basketry," as noted before. This craft proved to be very useful to him in making a living in later years when he became a Muslim. In Madaen also, he decided to make his living, just as he had done in Medina, after his emancipation, by selling the products of his manual skills such as baskets, bags, mats, fans, brooms, hangings, curtains and numerous other objects of household use - all made from palm-leaf and dried grass - the raw materials of his trade. He felt a strong aversion toward accepting even his own wages from the state exchequer which, he believed, belonged to the Muslims, and he was exceedingly squeamish about becoming a "burden" upon them.

* * * * *

During his incumbency as governor, Salman wished to demonstrate that the true message and mission of Islam was very broad in orientation and scope, and was not confined to an isolated thing called "religion," and that it was a way of life encompassing the whole range of thought, feeling, speech and deed. He believed that giving good administration to the Muslims was an act of Islamic piety, highly pleasing to Allah, and that it was his duty to give it to them. He equated the act of regulating the affairs of the Muslims with an act of devotion to Allah Himself.

But the Muslims were not to see their public affairs run by Salman, the friend and protege of their Prophet, Muhammed Mustafa (may Allah bless him and his Ahlel-Bayt).

Most unfortunately, Salman died within a few weeks after taking charge of his duties as governor of Madaen. His death was a personal loss to Ali ibn Abi Talib; but it was also a great and an irreparable loss to the whole Muslim umma. His death deprived the umma of his talents for administration in the Kingdom of Heaven on Earth which his master, Muhammed Mustafa, the

Messenger of Allah, had founded, and which Ali ibn Abi Talib had revived. Salman had been handpicked and groomed by Muhammed Mustafa himself.

As the governor of a province, Salman had the intent and the resolution of making Madaen a "show-place" where the Muslim umma would see a "chaste" government in action. It was his intent to demonstrate the practicability of the principles of the political philosophy of Quran Majid which Muhammed Mustafa, the Messenger of Allah, had taught him. He was very eager to show, to the poor and the weak of the Muslim umma, the compatibility of benevolence and power in his government.

With his death, a superb opportunity was lost forever.

Salman the Persian, the slave of Allah, and the bosom friend of Muhammed Mustafa and Ali ibn Abi Talib, died in A.D. 656 - within three months of the accession of Ali to the throne of caliphate, and within a few weeks of his own arrival in Madaen as its governor. He was 88 years old at his death, and was buried in Madaen.

May Allah be pleased with His loving slave, Salman el-Farsi, and may He overwhelm his soul with His Bounty, Grace and Mercy.

Chapter IX

Salman and the Prophets

There are astounding parallels between the life of Salman and the lives of three great prophets, viz., Abraham, Joseph son of Jacob, and Muhammed Mustafa the son of Abdullah, may Allah bless them all.

Abraham defied his father who was an idolater; Salman defied his father who was a fire-worshipper; and Muhammed Mustafa defied the Quraysh of Makkah who were polytheists. The reason for this defiance by all three of them was the same, viz., their faith in the Oneness of their Creator. Their pure faith as monotheists made conflict with the polytheists inevitable.

To all three of them, the lands of their birth proved to be inhospitable because of their faith, and all three of them had to forsake them. Abraham migrated from Iraq to Canaan (Palestine) and to Makkah; Salman migrated from Persia to Syria and to Yathrib; and Muhammed Mustafa migrated from Makkah to Medina. Each of them found his destiny in the land of his adoption.

Salman arrived in Yathrib many years before the arrival of Muhammed Mustafa in that city. For all those years, he was harassed, tormented and overworked by a pitiless, wanton and sadistic master, and he did not know a day of peace.

During the ten years before his migration to Yathrib, Muhammed Mustafa was also subject to harassment and persecution in Makkah by the pagans, and he too did not know a day of peace.

Thus, in the time-frame, the period of the persecution of Muhammed Mustafa by the Quraysh coincided with the period of the persecution of Salman by a Jew. They were both being persecuted at the same time.

* * * * *

Both Joseph, the apostle of Allah (may peace be upon him), and Salman (may Allah be pleased with him), were sold into slavery. Slavery was an exceedingly painful experience for them; yet they knew that Allah was with them. They trusted Allah entirely for their safety, and they allowed the sequence of events to evolve, as per His Great Design. Also, they did not let their adversity and personal grief blot out their awareness of Allah's control over their destiny at any time.

The faith of Joseph and Salman triumphed over adversity. There were many dark moments in which they felt utterly forlorn but those moments passed, and they recovered cheer and hope. How could they be forlorn when Allah's mercy was their constant companion, they realized.

A time came when they found their freedom - Joseph from prison and Salman from slavery. Each of them also found some other "treasures." Joseph found prophethood, and high rank in the government of Egypt. He used his new authority in the service of the suffering and toiling mass of humanity in Egypt. Salman found Muhammed Mustafa and Islam - the greatest of all treasures that any mortal could ever hope or wish to find.

* * * * *

Salman is also reminiscent of another Quranic figure - Luqman. Luqman was the great sage of antiquity. The 31st chapter of Quran is named after him. He is famous in the Muslim world for his homespun wisdom.

In his workaday life, at one time, Luqman was a slave and a craftsman. So was Salman.

Luqman overcame the temptation to become rich and powerful, even though he had the opportunity to become both. He refused worldly power and a kingdom when they were offered to him.

Salman too could have become rich and powerful but he too rose above temptation, and refused wealth and power.

Both Luqman and Salman chose for themselves lives of austerity and abstinence but they were not ascetics. They were puritanical without ever being ostentatious. The keynote of their lives was spontaneity, simplicity and freedom from affectation.

* * * * *

According to Luqman, human wisdom looks to Allah in true worship, seeking the light of guidance; and ennobles every act of life with true kindness to one's fellow human beings. Wisdom as expounded by him, is true service to Allah, and consists in moderation in all things.

To Luqman, as to Salman, true human wisdom was a part of Divine wisdom, and the two could not be separated. The beginning and the end of all wisdom, they believed, was conformity with the Will of Allah.

Luqman and Salman had the same outlook on life. This made them "philosophical allies" of each other even though they lived far apart from each other - hundreds of years in time and vast expanses of land in space.

May Allah be pleased with His slave, Salman who was endowed with many characteristics of the prophets and the sages but whose greatest pride was in being an 'ummatti' and a slave of

Muhammed Mustafa, the Messenger of Allah (may Allah bless him and his Ahlel-Bayt).

Chapter X

An Assessment of Salman's Philosophy of Life

Mr. Ali Shariati, the principal ideologist of radicalism in Iran in the 1970s, was a French-educated sociologist. He died in London in 1977. He pointed out in one of his works that the character and personality of Salman el-Farsi who was one of the greatest companions of the Prophet of Islam, were relatively unknown or were very little known in the Muslim world, and that he had not received the attention from the Muslim historians and biographers to which he was entitled in view of the high place he held in the sight of his master, Muhammed Mustafa, the Messenger of Allah (may Allah bless him and his Ahlel-Bayt).

Mr. Shariati considered the ignorance of many of the Muslims vis-a-vis the life of Salman, and the apparent lack of interest of the Muslim historians and biographers in him, deplorable, and said that the situation ought to be remedied since there was nothing commendable in ignorance. He further said that the modern historians ought to interpret the life of Salman in the light of his own ideals, and to rediscover the mainsprings of his deeds.

Salman belonged to the innermost circle of the companions of Muhammed Mustafa, the Messenger of Allah. The story of his life is immensely rich in inspirational lore. Would Muslims choose to live in ignorance about his life and his philosophy? If they do, the loss would be entirely theirs, and not his. If not, then their historians and biographers should address their talents to dispel this ignorance.

To the best of my knowledge and belief, no authoritative biography of Salman the Persian has so far been published in English, and it is a lamentable lack. Such information as is available on his life, is fragmentary and sketchy. It is my fervent hope that some day one of the young American Muslims will become the proud biographer of Salman el-Farsi, the personal friend and beloved of Muhammed Mustafa - the friend and beloved of Allah. The publication of his lifestory would be a great service, not only to the Muslims but also to the non-Muslims. The story of his life will inspire all those souls which are bewildered in their search for the answers to the riddles of life. At one time, Salman too was bewildered in search of those answers, and he too was in quest of the Light of Truth. Then he "discovered" Muhammed, and he found everything he had ever sought in his life.

Salman was the sign and the symbol of hope. He had held up hope in the midst of heartbreak and personal tragedy, and he was the emblem of constancy and faith. By dint of his piety and love, he found a place in the first rank of the slaves of Allah, and in the first rank of the friends of Muhammed Mustafa. This is and will remain an unchangeable fact. Therefore, if writers write Salman's life-story, and if readers read it, they would do so for their own edification.

* * * * *

Salman was not very anxious to "adjust," to compete and to accumulate. He did not make his principles "flexible" in order to "adjust," and he did not compete with anyone to get ahead in the "pecking order;" and he did not accumulate gold and silver as "hedges" against want and insecurity. He, in fact, had an almost excessive fear that they (gold and silver) would "contaminate" his life, and would tarnish its quality. He, therefore, deliberately made poverty the "staple" of his life.And he was not obsessed at any time with the ambition of acquiring political power. He showed himself consistently "allergic" to all those temptations.

Salman believed that if one devoted one's life to the acquisition of wealth and power, one almost inevitably forgot the poor and the weak members of the human family. Forgetting the poor and the weak, was, in his sight, an act of treason against Allah Himself. The central aim of his life was to keep in touch - constantly - with Allah. He lived in terror of losing that "touch" by neglecting, even momentarily, even inadvertently, the poor and the weak. He, therefore, did not allow the lust for riches and the temptation to become powerful, come between himself and the people who were poor and weak.

Salman, however, occupied himself with accumulating a very different kind of "wealth" - the pleasure of his Creator. How could he win His pleasure? For him the answer was obvious; he had to serve the most vulnerable members of the human family - the poor, the weak, the sick, the old, the disabled, the humble and those who "lead lives of quiet desperation." He devoted his life to their service with all his heart, mind, soul and body.

Salman wanted to experience the living reality of the Creator. He held the view that the Creator must be known in experience - not just by words or theory but by His Own Presence in one's life. He, therefore, gave form, structure and insight to his longing for his Creator by aligning himself with the crushed, the broken, the oppressed and the exploited members of the umma (=people) of his master, Muhammed Mustafa. In the age-old polarization of the rich and the poor, and the strong and the weak, he chose to be on the side of the poor and the weak. Perhaps he did so, not so much from free choice but from the inevitable propulsion of his nature. He was the "natural" ally and comrade-in-arms of the poor and the weak.

But in showing contempt for wealth and power, Salman was not advocating the philosophy of "retirement" from the world. The idea of "retirement" from the world and its problems is in conflict with the principles of Islam. He also remembered the maxim of his friend and master, Muhammed Mustafa (may Allah bless him and his Ahlel-Bayt), who said: "No monkery in Islam." He believed that monasticism and retirement from the world, were sterile and morbid experiments with the great gift of life, and instinctively rejected them. His philosophy was a direct antithesis of the philosophy of escapism.

Salman rejected monasticism as a way of life, just as, earlier, he had rejected hedonism and sybaritism as a way of life. The only good life, and the only truly happy life, he maintained, was the one lived in obedience to the commandments of Allah. The key to everlasting happiness and success in this world and in the Hereafter, according to him, was in total surrender to Allah - a surrender full of humility, hope, happiness and love.

For Salman, life's true meaning sprang from the heart and the soul; from beliefs and purposes larger than one's individual life, and from a sense of direction in it. The beliefs and purposes of life were revealed to him by Muhammed Mustafa; and he found direction in it in the "compass" encased in Quran Majid.

If there are any two words which would sum up Salman's whole philosophy of life, they are Love and Service. What kept him alive, was the Love of Allah and His Messenger, Muhammed Mustafa; their love fed the flame of his life. And he was at his very best when he was giving Service - to his fellow human beings. Love-and-Service were the raison d'etre of Salman's whole existence.

As noted before, Muhammed Mustafa, the Messenger of Allah, himself had inducted Salman into Islam in A.D. 622. With the blessing of Islam, Salman had also received the honor of his

(Muhammed's) companionship. This means that the companionship of Muhammed Mustafa and Salman lasted for ten years - until the former's death in A.D. 632. Those were the happiest and the most fruitful years of Salman's long life. In those ten years of blessings unlimited, he found recompense for all the setbacks of life. From the moment, his first glance fell on the radiant visage of Muhammed Mustafa (may Allah bless him and his Ahlel-Bayt), he lived a rich, abundant and rewarding life, basking every moment in the Grace and Mercy of Allah, and in the glow of the friendship of Muhammed Mustafa.

* * * * *

The antecedents of Salman the Persian may have been alien (non-Arab), but he was an authentic Islamic "original," such as few others among his contemporaries were.

* * * * *

How did Salman adjudge his own life? This question was never posed to him. But we know that he had two dominant aims in life, and he was consistently consistent in pursuing them. The first of them was to discover the Eternal and the Ultimate Truths revealed by the Creator to mankind, and he discovered them in Quran Majid. He found Allah's purpose in creating man stated implicitly and explicitly in Quran Majid. His second aim was to serve Muhammed Mustafa - the Bringer and the Interpreter of Quran Majid, and he did. He realized both aims in life. He must, therefore, have considered his life to be eminently successful.

* * * * *

In A.D. 624 Salman was still a slave but it was one of the happiest years of his life. Two important events took place in that year which brought happiness to him and to his master, Muhammed Mustafa (may Allah bless him and his Ahlel-Bayt).

The first of these two events was the battle of Badr. Badr was the first test of strength - on the battlefield - of Islam and paganism. Allah, in His mercy, was pleased to bestow victory upon Islam.

Following is a brief account of the Battle of Badr.

In early March 624 reports were received in Medina that a caravan of the Quraysh was returning to Makkah from Syria. According to these reports, the caravan was carrying not only merchandise but also weapons, which together with the profits of the trade, computed at the time at 50,000 dinars, were to be used in a campaign against the Muslims. The caravan was led by Abu Sufyan, the chief of the clan of Bani Umayya in Makkah.

Muhammed Mustafa decided to intercept the Makkan caravan. He appointed Abu Lababa the governor of Medina, and left the city with a force of 313 men. Of these, 80 were Muhajirs (Immigrants from Makkah), and 233 were the Ansaris (citizens of Madina). Their destination was Badr, a village 50 miles south-west of Medina where they expected to make contact with the caravan from Syria.

In the meantime, the Makkan spies informed Abu Sufyan also 'that a body of Muslims was moving toward his caravan. As soon as he heard this report, he abandoned the customary caravan route, led the caravan westward to the Red Sea coast, and then turned south toward Makkah via an off-beat track. He also sent a messenger to Makkah asking for aid. In Makkah, Abu Jahl, an arch-enemy of Muhammed and Islam, eagerly responded to the appeal of Abu Sufyan, and marched out with a force of 1000 warriors against the Muslims. A train of 700 camels carried materials for war and other supplies. The infantry was wearing chain-mail and armor.

When the Prophet of Islam arrived in the environs of Badr, he sent Ali ibn Abi Talib to reconnoiter the surrounding country. Ali surprised some water-carriers of the enemy at a well, and brought them before the Prophet. From them he learned that the caravan of the Quraysh had already escaped, and that an army of invasion from Makkah, marching on Medina, was encamped at that very moment behind the nearby hills.

Sir William Muir

> On reaching the neighbourhood of Badr, Mohammed sent forward Ali, with a few others, to reconnoitre the rising ground above the springs. There they surprised three water-carriers of the enemy, as they were about to fill their sheepskins. One escaped to the Coreish; the other two were captured and taken to the Moslem army. From them Mohammed discovered the proximity of the enemy. There were 950 men; more than three-fold the number of the Moslem army. They were mounted on 700 camels and 100 horses, the horsemen all clad in mail.

(The Life of Mohammed, 1877, p. 230)

The presence of an active, aggressive and menacing army, instead of a rich caravan, within close proximity, changed the entire situation for the Muslims, and a fresh assessment of the perils and possibilities had to be made. The Muslims were very poorly equipped. The Prophet held a council of war and put the matter before his companions to consider and to adopt the course of action to be taken.

The Prophet was especially anxious to know if the Ansar would be willing to fight outside Medina. The leaders of the Ansar assured him that they would obey him and follow him in war just as they obeyed him and followed him in peace, and that he would not find in them hesitation of any kind in carrying out his orders.

The declaration of support by the Ansar was forthright and unequivocal which pleased the Prophet, and he invoked the blessings of God upon them. He knew that neither the battle of Badr nor any other battle could be fought without the whole-hearted support of the Ansar. The Ansar were, in fact, indispensable for success in the struggle between Islam and paganism.

The Muslims were united. Though materially and numerically they were at a disadvantage, their unity and singleness of purpose were going to be a source of immense strengh to them in the forthcoming contest with the Makkan army.

Muhammed Mustafa, the Messenger of Allah, himself and all the rank-and-file Muslims were aware that the outcome of the contest with the foe on the following day, would be overwhelming in its effects. They knew in fact that the contest would change the course of history forever.

Sir William Muir

> Mohammed was fully alive to the critical situation. The fate of Islam hung upon the issue of the approaching battle.

> (The Life of Mohammed, 1877, p. 233)

The battle of Badr was fought on Friday, the 17th of Ramadhan of the second year of Hijra, a date that corresponds to March 15, 624. Early in the morning, the Makkan army moved out of its camp to meet the Muslims. The two armies ranged themselves in battle formation. Abu Jahl rode in front of his army reviewing the deployment of the infantry and the disposition of the cavalry, and making last-minute changes where necessary.

The Muslims did not have a cavalry, and the infantry was not well-armed. But their morale was high. Muhammed Mustafa took a bow in his hand, and went from one end of the rows to the other, straightening them. His last act before the beginning of the hostilities, was to pray to Allah to grant victory to His faithful slaves.

The battle began in the traditional Arab manner of warfare in which a champion of one side rode or stepped out of his line, and challenged the heroes of the enemy to meet him in single combat. This gave him an opportunity to win personal glory by showing his own bravery, strength, horsemanship and skill in archery, and versatility in the use of sword, spear and other weapons. After these initial duels, it was customary for the two armies to charge at each other, and to engage in hand-to-hand fighting.

From the Makkan army, three champions, Utbah the son of Rabia; Shaiba, his brother; and Walid, his son; came out into the open space between the two armies and challenged the Muslims. Their challenge was taken up, in the camp of Islam, by Hamza, the uncle of Muhammed and Ali; Obeida ibn al-Harith, a cousin of Muhammed and Ali; and Ali ibn Abi Talib.

Ali's adversary was Walid bin Utbah, one of the fiercest warriors of the Quraysh. They were the youngest pair, and they were the first to engage in fighting. The other two pairs paused, to watch the young warriors in action. The two young men exchanged blows for a few minutes and then Ali struck a blow which killed Walid. Thereupon, the other warriors also charged at each other. Hamza killed Utbah but Obeida was mortally wounded by Shaiba. When Ali saw Obeida collapsing, he attacked Shaiba and killed him also. With all three of their opponents dead, and no one else in the field, Ali and Hamza carried Obeida back into the Muslim lines.

Obeida ibn al-Harith, the first cousin of Muhammed and Ali ibn Abi Talib, died from loss of blood. He was the first Muslim to be killed in the battle-field, and this makes him the Protomartyr

of the campaigns of Islam. May Allah's boundless mercy overwhelm his noble soul.

Sir William Muir

> The two brothers, Shaiba and Otba, and Walid, the
> son of Otba, advanced into the space between the
> armies, and defied three champions from the army of
> Mohammed to meet them singly. Mohammed, turning
> to his kinsmen, said: Ye, sons of Hashim! Arise and
> fight, according to your right.' Then Hamza, Obeida,
> and Ali, the uncle and cousins of the Prophet, went
> forth. Hamza wore an ostrich feather in his breast and
> a while plume distinguished the helmet of Ali.
> Then Otba called on his son, Walid, Arise and fight.'
> So Walid stepped forth and Ali came out against him.
> They were the youngest of the six. The combat was
> short; Walid fell mortally wounded by the sword of
> Ali.
> (The Life of Mohammed, 1877, p. 234)

* * * * *

Badr was the first encounter, on the battle-field, between
Islam and paganism.It was opened, on the side of Islam, by Ali
ibn Abi Talib, the Lion of Allah; and his victory foreshadowed
the eventual triumph of Islam in its ten-year-long conflict with
the polytheists of Arabia. All other battles of Islam followed the
same pattern; Ali was the victor in every one of them.

* * * * *

When all three heroes of the Quraysh were slain, Abu Jahl,

their general, did not send any more champions to challenge the Muslims. He decided against taking any further chances with Ali and Hamza, and he ordered his troops to advance. The Makkans charged the Muslims in a well-coordinated attack but could not break their formations which held firm under the command of Ali and Hamza. The Makkans were regrouping for a new attack when the Prophet signalled the Muslims to charge. Ali and Hamza led the Muslim counter-charge, and both of them carried slaughter and dismay into the thickest of the enemy ranks. Many of the Makkan leaders and officers were killed, among them Abu Jahl himself. He was killed by two young men of the Ansar. After his death, the Quraysh were unable to regroup and they began to retreat. The Muslims pressed their advantage and the Makkan retreat soon turned into a rout.

Islam had won its first and its most important victory!

Abu Jahl was one of the most implacable, unconscionable and rabid foes of Muhammed Mustafa and Islam. From the moment, Muhammed had unfurled the banner of Tauheed in Makkah, Abu Jahl had sworn eternal hostility to him and to the Principle of Tauheed, and he never veered from that aim. Of all the idolaters of Makkah, he was the most presumptuous and the most cruel; but he met his nemesis in the Battle of the Badr. He had lived and he died with evil.

D. S. Margoliouth

It certainly appears that the winning of this most important fight was in the main due to the prowess of Ali and Hamza. The Prophet is said to have bestowed especial praise on the valour of Simak s/o Kharashah; Sahl s/o Hunaif; al-Harith s/o al-Simmah; and Kais s/o al-Rabi; all of them Medinese.

(Mohammed and the Rise of Islam, 1931, pp. 260-261)

114

Tor Andre

> By noon the battle was over. The Quraysh fled. Forty-nine of the enemy had fallen and Ali had killed 22, either alone or with the help of others. An equal number was captured. The believers had lost 14 men on the field of battle.
>
> (Mohammed, the Man and his Faith, 1960, pp. 145-146)

As noted above, Badr is the most important battle in the whole history of Islam, and one of the most important in world history. Victory in Badr guaranteed the existence of Islam, and the physical survival of the Muslim community of Medina which heretofore had appeared, at best, to be precarious.

R. A. Nicholson

> But the importance of Mohammed's success (in the battle of Badr) cannot be measured by the material damage he inflicted (upon the pagans of Mecca). Considering the momentous issues involved, we must allow that Badr, like Marathon, is one of the greatest and most memorable battles in all history.
>
> (A Literary History of the Arabs, 1969, p. 174)

* * * * *

The architect of the victory of Islam at Badr, beyond any question, was Ali ibn Abi Talib. In his authoritative Life of *the Prophet* (Urdu), M. Shibli, the Indian historian, calls Ali the Hero of the Battle of Badr.

It appears that Ali was chosen expressly by Allah to be His "instrument" of victory. Ali was Allah's "instrument" of victory

115

in the battle of Badr, and in every subsequent battle, and each time he brought glory, honor and victory to Islam.

F. E. Peters says in his book, *Allah's Commonwealth*, that the leadership at Mecca was permanently crippled after the battle of Badr.

The leadership of the Quraysh was in fact permanently crippled at Badr, and it was Ali's sword which made it a cripple. He alone killed 22 Makkans, twelve of them being the leading members of the clan of Bani Umayya. The rest of the army of Islam killed another 27 idolaters. At this time Ali was 24 years old.

* * * * *

Among the spoils of the battle of Badr there was a sword which was to become the most famous sword in the whole history of Islam. Its name was Dhul-Fiqar.

Washington Irving

Among the spoils of the battle of Badr was a famous sword of admirable temper called Dhul-Fiqar, or the Piercer. Mohammed ever afterwards bore it when in battle, and his son-in-law, Ali, inherited it at his death. (The Life of Mohammed)

Robert Payne

Meanwhile there was the booty (of the battle of Badr) to be attended to: a great treasure consisting of 150 camels and horses together with vast quantities of vestment and armor. A number of swords was captured, among them a strange double-pointed sword which came to be known as Dhu'l-Fiqar, or "Cleaver of Vertebrae." Muhammad wore it during all his subse-

116

quent battles, and seems to have believed that the possession of this sword was the demonstrable sign of inevitable victory. In time the sword was inherited by Ali, and many copies were made engraved with the words "No sword can match the Cleaver, and no young knight can compare with Ali."

(The Holy Sword)

After the battle of Badr, Ali fought all the battles of Islam with Dhul-Fiqar. In his hand, it became the "Piercer" of the heart of Kufr (paganism), and the "Cleaver" of the back of Shirk (Polytheism). In his hand, it became the Messenger of Death for the pagans and the polytheists. In his hand, it became the Destroyer of rebellion against Allah Ta'ala, and of defiance to His Messenger, Muhammed Mustafa.

* * * * *

(The battle of Badr is called *Furqan*, in verses 29 and 41 of the eighth chapter (Anfal) of Quran Majid because it was the first trial of strength by battle, in Islam, between the powers of good and evil. *Furqan* is the Criterion between right and wrong, decision between the forces of faith and unbelief. A. Yusuf Ali).

Victory at Badr invested Islam with immense prestige. It was the most important factor in the consolidation of Islam. It enabled Muhammed Mustafa to lay the foundations of the first and the last Kingdom of Heaven on Earth.

D. S. Margoliouth

No event in the history of Islam was of more importance than this battle (Badr): Koran rightly calls it the Day of Deliverance, the day before which the Moslems were weak, after which they were strong. Wealth, fame, honor, power, all of them were secured or at any

rate brought within reach by the Day of Deliverance.
(Mohammed and the Rise of Islam, 1931, p. 269)

* * * * *

As noted before, Salman had not been able to take part in the battle of Badr. His master did not allow him to leave the oasis. Salman spent many moments of anguish, suspense and torment. But then he turned to a Source of strength and comfort which had never failed him; he prayed to Allah to send His "reinforcements" to His slaves - the Muslims - and to give them victory. When Allah was pleased to give victory to the Muslims, Salman rejoiced, and he knew that the survival of Islam was guaranteed. Victory of Badr was, in fact, a "personal assurance" to him that Islam, his beloved Islam, was, and would remain viable for all time. He thanked Allah for the great Gift of Victory in the Battle of Badr. He knew that he - a humble slave of Allah and His Messenger - also had a share in that glorious Gift.

* * * * *

Salman identified himself both with the triumphs of Muhammed Mustafa such as the Battle of Badr, and with his reverses such as the battle of Uhud. Muhammed's happiness was his happiness, and Muhammed's sorrow was his sorrow. Faith in the infallible leadership of Muhammed, in this world and in the world to come, and constancy to the principles of Islam, were the ideological underpinnings of his philosophy of life.

* * * * *

The second event that brightened the year 624 for Salman, was the marriage of Hadhret Fatima Zahra, the daughter of Muhammed Mustafa, the Messenger of Allah, and Ali ibn Abi Talib. Their marriage was solemnized two months after the battle of Badr.

* * * * *

On the first of Zilhajj (the 12th month of the Islamic calendar) of 2 A.H. (A.D. 624), Muhammed Mustafa, the Messenger of Allah, invited the Muslims of Medina, to attend a banquet in the Great Mosque, on the blessed occasion of the marriage of his daughter, Fatima Zahra, and Ali ibn Abi Talib, the Architect of Victory in the Battle of Badr.

When all the guests had arrived and were seated, Muhammed Mustafa, the Messenger of Allah, greeted them. He praised and thanked Allah for His blessings and His mercy, and read selected passages from Quran Majid. After this exordium, he read the Sermon of the marriage of Ali and Fatima; declared them husband and wife; and invoked upon both of them, the blessings and the mercy of Allah.

All the guests congratulated Muhammed Mustafa on this most auspicious of all occasions. Salman was foremost among them. His master had allowed him to attend the wedding ceremonies. After the ceremonies, the guests feasted upon bread, lamb meat, milk and date fruit.

* * * * *

On the 24th of Zilhajj, Fatima Zahra had to bid farewell to her parental home so she could go to the house of her husband. Muhammed Mustafa, the Messenger of Allah, aided her in entering the howdah of his she-camel. Medina rang with the shouts of Allah-o-Akbar (=Allah is Great). The wedding procession was then ready to march.

In the lead of the procession were all the wives of Muhammed Mustafa, the Messenger of Allah. They were the "mothers of the believers." They were reciting verses in praise of Allah. Just behind them, was the she-camel carrying the howdah of the bride. It was Salman el-Farsi who held the reins of the she-camel in his hand. He too was reading passages from Quran Majid.

The she-camel carrying the howdah of the bride, was advancing toward the destination at a leisurely pace. Muhammed Mustafa, the father of the bride, walked on the right side of the she-camel; and his uncle, Hamza, the Lion of Allah, walked on the left. All the young men of Bani Hashim (the clan of Muhammed Mustafa) rode their proud steeds, as they escorted the bride. Their gleaming swords were held high over their heads.

Behind the contingent of Beni Hashim, there were the Muhajir and the Ansar women. They were quietly reading Islamic devotionals. The last "contingent" was made up of the Muhajireen and the Ansar themselves. They were all chanting hymns to the glory of Allah. Their recital was punctuated from time to time by the thunderous shouts of Allah-o-Akbar (=Allah is Great).

This heavenly procession made a circuit of the Great Mosque of Medina, and then halted at its destination - the house of the bridegroom, Ali ibn Abi Talib. Muhammed Mustafa, the Messenger of Allah, aided his daughter in alighting from the howdah. He then held her hand, and symbolically placed it in the hand of her husband-Ali ibn Abi Talib, and then standing at the threshold of the house, said the following prayer:

> "O Allah! O Sovereign of the Universe! All praise and thanks belong to Thee. I commend Fatima and Ali, Thy loving slaves, to Thy protection. Be Thou their Protector. Be pleased with them. Show them Thy pleasure. Bestow upon them Thy boundless bounty, grace and mercy. Bestow upon them Thy best rewards. Make their marriage happy and fruitful, and make both of them steadfast in Thy love and in Thy service."

* * * * *

Muhammed Mustafa, the Messenger of Allah, had called Salman a member of his own family. It was the most sacrosanct family in all creation. Its members were the chosen ones of Allah Himself. As noted before, Salman shared all the sweets and bitters of life with them; he rejoiced in their happiness, and he reacted to their sorrows with the same intensity as they did.

The day Fatima Zahra and Ali ibn Abi Talib were married, was one of the happiest and most memorable days in the life of Salman the Persian.

It was the pleasure and the decree of Allah Himself that Fatima Zahra, the daughter of His Messenger, and Ali ibn Abi Talib, His devout slave, should be married. It was, therefore, an occasion of profound satisfaction and happiness for both of His slaves - Muhammed and Salman - to see Fatima Zahra and Ali ibn Abi Talib - united in holy wedlock, as per the pleasure and decree of Allah.

* * * * *

They wished for themselves nothing except what Allah wished for them.

BUT YE SHALL NOT WILL EXCEPT AS ALLAH WILLS, THE CHERISHER OF THE WORLDS.
(Quran Majid. Chapter 81; verse 29)

Supreme felicity came for Muhammed Mustafa and Salman from the knowledge that they carried out the wishes of their Creator, and did their utmost to win His pleasure. This eagerness to serve Him, was what set them apart, in His sight, from other mortals. Through love and service they became His favorites.

* * * * *

May Allah bless Muhammed Mustafa, Fatima Zahra, Ali ibn Abi Talib, their children, and their faithful friend, Salman the Persian.

The following verses of Quran Majid are addressed to those sincere and loving slaves of Allah who put His pleasure ahead of their own pleasure. Salman the Persian was one of the foremost of those slaves:

(To the soul of the righteous will be said);
"O THOU SOUL, IN (COMPLETE) REST AND SATIS-FACTION! COME BACK TO THY LORD, - WELL-PLEASED (THYSELF) AND WELL-PLEASED UNTO HIM! ENTER THOU, THEN, AMONG MY DEVOTEES! YEA, ENTER THOU MY HEAVEN!"

(Chapter 89; verses 27-30)

* * * * *

May Allah bless Salman el-Farsi, and may He elevate him to the highest ranks in the hierarchy of His true and faithful friends. Salman's greatest pleasure in this world was to wait on Him; his greatest pleasure in the Hereafter also, will be the same.

* * * * *

May Allah bestow His grace and His blessings upon His Messenger, Muhammed Mustafa, and his Ahlel-Bayt. It was through him that Salman el-Farsi received the blessing and the light of Islam.

* * * * *

New York
January 8, 1988

BIBLIOGRAPHY

Quran Majid (English translation by A. Yusuf Ali)
Rasul-i-Rahmet (Urdu) by M. Abul Kalam Azad
Dalael an-Nubuwwa (Arabic) by Bayhaqi
Sahih (Traditions) (Arabic) by Imam Bukhari
Suwar min Hayat er-Rasul (Arabic) by Amin Dawidar
Siyar Aa'lam an Nubalaa (Arabic) by Imam Dhahabi
The Encyclopaedia Britannica
The Encyclopaedia of Islam
The Decline and Fall of the Roman Empire by Edward Gibbon
The Great Arab Conquests by Lt.General Sir John Glubb
Al-Bidaya wan-Nihaya (Arabic) by Imam ibn Kathir
Mohammed and the Rise of Islam by D. S. Margoliouth
Hayat Muhammed (Arabic) by Muhammed Husayn Haykal
The Life of the Messenger of Allah (Arabic) by Muhammed
ibn Ishaq
The Life of Mohammed by Sir William Muir
Sahih (Traditions) (Arabic) by Imam Muslim
A Literary History of the Arabs by R. A. Nicholson
Mabsut (Arabic) by Sarakhsi
The Life of the Apostle of God (Urdu) by M. Shibli
Mohammed, the Man and his Faith, by Tor Andre
Kitab al-Maghazi (Arabic) by Muhammed ibn Umar al-Waqidi